# Mountain Biking in the Bay Area

# Mountain Biking in the Bay Area

A Nearly Complete Guide

Michael Hodgson
&
Mark Lord

Western Tanager Press
Santa Cruz

Cover illustration by Jim M'Guiness
Cover design by Lynn Piquett
Maps by Phyllis Wright and Lynn Piquett
Photographs by the authors
Typography by TypaGraphix

ISBN: 0-934136-51-3

Library of Congress Card Catalog Number: 92-62542

Printed in the United States of America

Western Tanager Press
1111 Pacific Avenue
Santa Cruz, CA 95060

To our wives, Karen Samford and Sandy Lord, for enduring and understanding our need to write and ride. We are ceaselessly amazed, in debt, and in love with their desire to support and share in our dreams. For continuing to understand muddy floors, push our frustrated minds, soothe our sore muscles, and give up your time for ours, we dedicate this second book to you.

# Acknowledgements

This book is the continuation of a dream that both of us have shared over the years, the dream of being authors and writing about that which we love. However this book would never have seen completion without the support and guidance of many wonderful people: park rangers, friends, and loved ones. We are very indebted to the following:

Sharee Eisinga and John Pannozo
Elliott and Hillary Dubreuil
Responsible Organized Mountain Pedalers of Campbell, CA.
Raleigh Bicycles
Jay and Shirley Supkoff
Bud and Norma Lord
Peter and Mary Hodgson
Jay and Shirley Supkoff
John and Ande Clapp
Tanner Girard
Doc Wanamaker
Doug Bender and Mindi Lord
Skeets, Concha, Merritt, and Spencer Lord
John, Debbie and Lauren Emerson
Todd Vogel
Shaws Lighweight Cyclery
The folks at Catalyst Consulting
Bill Sunderland
Publisher Hal Morris
Editor Michael Gant
Rangers Keenen Sederquist, Joe Collins and Al Blum at Wilder Ranch
Mark McCarroll
All of the rangers and volunteers who responded to our inquiries concerning the status of their trails
And especially to Sandy Lord for all of her hours spent on the telephone and computer trying to make some sense of our text.

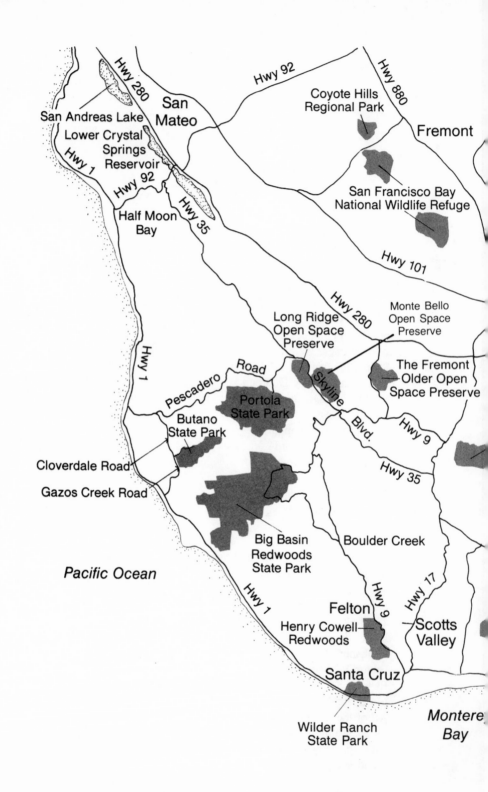

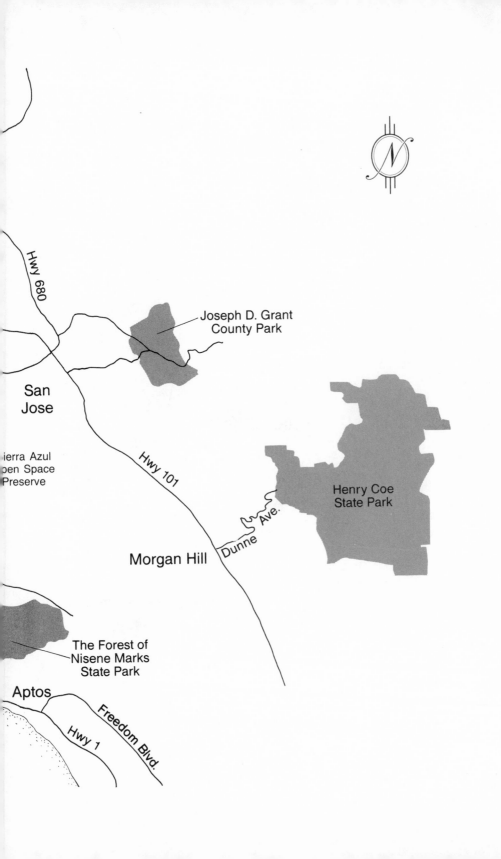

Hwy 680

Joseph D. Grant
County Park

San
Jose

ierra Azul
pen Space
Preserve

Hwy 101

Henry Coe
State Park

Dunne Ave.

Morgan Hill

The Forest of
Nisene Marks
State Park

Aptos

Freedom Blvd.

Hwy 1

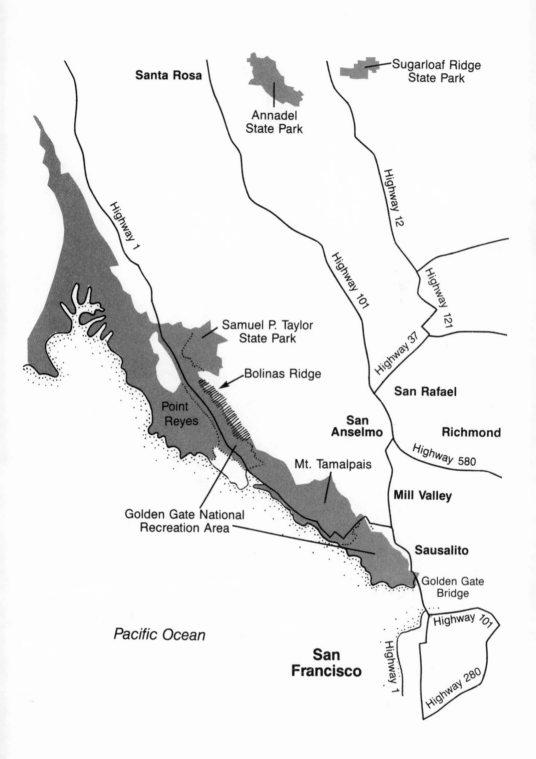

Santa Rosa

Sugarloaf Ridge
State Park

Annadel
State Park

Highway 1

Highway 12

Highway 101

Highway 121

Highway 37

Samuel P. Taylor
State Park

Bolinas Ridge

San Rafael

Point
Reyes

San
Anselmo

Richmond

Highway 580

Mt. Tamalpais

Mill Valley

Golden Gate National
Recreation Area

Sausalito

Golden Gate
Bridge

Pacific Ocean

Highway 101

Highway 1

San
Francisco

Highway 280

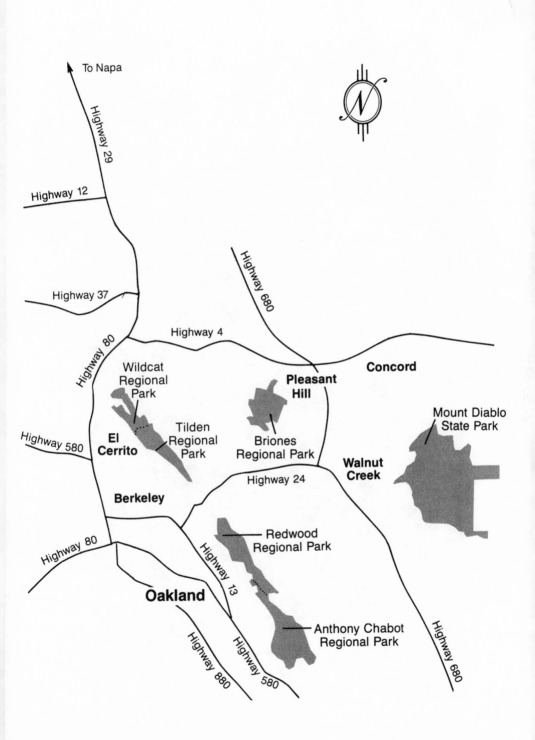

# Contents

# Preface

Since the publication of our first mountain biking book back in 1989, the world of mountain biking has continued to grow, and with that growth continued to experience a world of growing pains. Fortunately, the vast majority of visitors to the backcountry trails of the Bay Area are there for the same reason I am, to experience the serenity of pedaling through woods and meadows for the sheer joy of it.

The memory of seeing a bobcat fade into the trees not more than 15 yards away from me back in 1989 is still etched in my mind. Since then, I have been blessed with many more wonderful and memorable mountain biking experiences. I use my bike less and less now for gut-wrenching, heart-pounding workouts and more for a way to find time to coast quietly and listen to the world around me. It remains true that although I pedal far less than I used to, I have and continue to be able to view far more than I ever would have dreamed possible.

My joy with biking, however, is tempered with a hint of frustration and sadness (see the reprint in the Appendix of my article that appeared in the *San Jose Mercury News*). Illegal and irresponsible riding continues to cause land managers grief, often resulting in the ultimate slap to all mountain bikers—a closed trail. It is not just the oft-mentioned teenage renegades or gonzo mountain bike racers either. I have witnessed numerous infractions of rules and etiquette by well-outfitted middle-aged men and women who really should know better. Wake up gang!

I once said that the dirt roads and jeep trails that crisscross the Bay Area are the "E Tickets" to a backyard filled with more wonders than you've ever imagined. E Ticket, however, implies a roller-coaster, need-for-speed mentality and that is as out of place on any trail as an automobile. Save your speed demon runs for a sanctioned race—there are enough of them to quench most appetites.

The mountain bike is an excellent way to socially and peacefully enjoy the green belt that surrounds our Bay Area. There is a lot to explore and you can't possibly do it in a weekend. Take your time, ride safely, ride responsibly, have fun and keep your eyes open. Maybe I'll see you on the trail!

MICHAEL HODGSON

In the four years since I wrote the last preface, much has changed, both for me and for the status of mountain biking. I've gained the wonderful addition of a daughter and all of the joys and frustrations of parenthood, mountain biking has also grown up somewhat and gained some respectability, at least in some people's eyes.

I no longer have the time or flexibility to drop everything and go exploring on my mountain bike at a moment's notice; more and more these days I am revisiting my favorite backcountry spots with my daughter towed along in her trailer. I've found that I may have missed what was right in front of my nose: the blue-bellied lizard or periwinkle or trail of ants that cross the trail; now my daughter's curiosity calls my attention to these finer details.

Sometimes as adults we're so intent on trying to extract the most intense experiences from the world around us that we miss some very important occurrences — the soaring of a red-tailed hawk overhead, the gentle breeze as it blows and tousles the golden grasses, the play of light shimmering on an expanse of blue water.

I still enjoy the thrill of a rush down a technical trail and the giddy, lightheaded feeling after a long and strenuous uphill, but my daughter has also reintroduced me to the other, more subtle aspects of the world too — those that have gone about their wonderful business long before we even thought of the wheel; with luck, it will all be here long after our iron steeds are bits of rust.

Be responsible enough to realize that others also want to see that which we've been lucky enough to experience — spend some time giving back by working to acquire more public land or spending a day rebuilding an eroded trail. Go enjoy and explore this beautiful land that surrounds us.

MARK LORD

# Introduction

Mountain biking is a sport generating much controversy. Understandably, a pedal-powered vehicle that goes virtually anywhere is enough to thrill the most adventurous of souls yet send shudders down the spine of many wilderness purists. It's not hard to imagine a hiker's anger at being startled out of a peaceful, contemplative state by an out-of-control, mach-speed mountain biker. Yet, it is also not hard to imagine the joy of quietly pedaling along a ridge by way of a jeep trail bathed in early morning light.

A weekend visit to Mount Tamalpais is testament to the fact that too much publicity on one area can produce catastrophic results. There are hundreds of miles of fire roads in the Bay Area, many that seldom have more than a few visitors at one time. While we have no intention of exploiting coveted trails purposely kept "secret" by locals, we do wish to increase awareness of the vast wealth of mountain biking adventure to be had virtually outside our back door.

We hope to relieve the congestion of some areas and ensure continued mountain biking access in regions that are in need of public awareness. We have no interest in promoting growth in mountain biking in areas that are overcrowded, ecologically fragile, or political hotbeds of contention, nor do we condone their destruction. There is more than enough land for the hiker, equestrian, and mountain biker to coexist peacefully. Our purpose is to write a guide book that is responsible in its presentation.

The Bay Area is bordered by numerous open spaces, preserves, and regional and state parks; many of these areas are mountainous and blessed with a vastness that can make access difficult by foot. Frequently a trailhead's immediate vicinity is crowded with hikers, although only a few miles distant the same trail is deserted. Mountain bikes provide a means to reach a destination in several hours that would take more than a day to reach on foot. An all-terrain bicycle, in the hands of a responsible user, becomes a legitimate tool for exploring the backwoods and foothills. Perhaps we can help others to discover the beauty that exists just beyond our back door.

Despite the rumors and image projected by some, mountain biking is not just for the brave few willing to endure bone-jarring descents and breakneck speed. Mountain biking is to be enjoyed at any speed, even if you have to get off and walk for awhile. We've included rides that range from flat and easy to steep and strenuous. No matter what your mountain biking abilities, you may find yourself discovering wild places you never dreamed possible.

Mountain biking is as varied as those that partake in it. It is a dry-land version of backcountry skiing or a quiet encounter with nature. It is a morning ride through a valley shrouded in mist or a zigzag descent to a river swimming hole. It is a social outing spent with family or friends or a personal experience with only you and the breeze in your ears. Whatever you desire, you will find something in mountain biking for you.

In the following pages, we will take you on a journey of the Bay Area mountains and foothills. We have tried very hard to give you a sampling of the joy of mountain biking in a variety of areas. Although every ride we describe in this guide was legal at the time of printing, it is possible that any trail could be closed to mountain bikes at any time. The park services may opt to close a trail because of overuse, erosion, or political pressure. Please, if any trail or road displays this sign (bike symbol), even if described in this guide, respect the ruling and don't do more to ruin the image of mountain biking by riding the trail.

It is our hope that you will experience much joy and discovery with our guide. However, this is just a starting point. There is so much more out there than we could or wanted to include. The rest is up to you.

### Responsible Organized Mountain Pedalers Cyclists Code

The following is a list of "rules of conduct" for all mountain bikers to abide by. It is provided by R.O.M.P., Responsible Organized Mountain Pedalers of Campbell, California. For more information about this non-profit group, call 408-356-8230 or write P.O. Box 1723, Campbell, CA 95009-1723. "Thousands of miles of dirt trails have been closed to mountain bicycling because of the irresponsible riding habits of a few riders. Do your part to maintain trail access by observing the following rules."

### Rules of the Trail

1. RIDE ON OPEN TRAILS ONLY: Respect trail and road closures (ask if not sure), avoid possible trespass on private land, and obtain permits and authorization as may be required. Federal and State Wilderness Areas are closed to cycling. Additional trails may be closed because of sensitive environmental concerns or conflicts with other users. Your riding example will determine what is closed to all cyclists.

2. LEAVE NO TRACE: Be sensitive to the dirt beneath you. You should not ride—even on open trails—under conditions where you will leave evidence of your passing, such as on certain soils shortly after a rain. Observe the different types of soils and trail construction and practice minimum-impact cycling. This also means staying on the trail and not creating any new ones. Be sure to pack out at least as much as you pack into an area.

3. CONTROL YOUR BICYCLE: Inattention even for a second can cause disaster for yourself or others. Excessive speed maims and threatens people; there is no excuse for it.

4. ALWAYS YIELD TRAIL: Make known your approach well in advance. A friendly greeting (or bell) is considerate and works well; startling someone may cause loss of trail access. Show your respect when passing others by slowing to a walk or stopping all together. Anticipate that other trail users may be around corners or blind spots.

5. NEVER SPOOK ANIMALS: All animals are startled by an unannounced approached, a sudden movement, or a loud noise. This can be dangerous for you, others, and the animals. Give animals extra room and time to adjust to you. In passing, use special care and follow the directions of horseback riders (ask if uncertain). Running cattle and disturbing wild animals is a serious offense. Leave gates as you found them or as marked.

6. PLAN AHEAD: Know your equipment, your ability, and the area in which you are riding and prepare accordingly. Be self-sufficient at all times, keep your machine in good repair, carry necessary supplies for changes in the weather or other conditions. A well-executed trip is a satisfaction to you and not a burden or offense to others. Keep trails open by setting an example of responsible cycling for all mountain bicyclists.

# Basic Biking Technique

Although power, strength, and endurance have their place in mountain biking, finesse and balance are a good rider's main emphasis. Most difficult terrain and trail hazards are best maneuvered at steady speeds and in low gears. In all situations, concentrate on smooth transitions and shift gears aggressively. Anticipating upcoming gear changes is the key to successfully negotiating mountain biking's ups and downs.

Musicians and artists may speak of their instruments being extensions of themselves; the same is true for mountain bikers (think of yourself as the Casals of mountain biking). Visualizing your metallic steed as a tool instead of a bicycle might help you to think of it as an extension of your lower body. Proficient mountain bikers can negotiate some seemingly fantastic objects: fallen logs, boulders, deep streams, sometimes even all three at the same time (just kidding). They've ceased to think about what to do with their bikes and instead think of how to position their bodies. Very slight repositioning of hips or knees or transitioning weight from back to front or side can have remarkable (and sometimes unexpected) results.

UPHILL RIDING: For uphills, always start in the lowest gear; it is easier to shift up than down. Steeper hills increase the feeling of an unweighted front wheel. Compensate for this by slightly shifting weight forward. You must be careful not to unweight the rear wheel so much that you lose traction. A technique that works well on very steep hills is to slightly to rock your weight back and forth; this prevents wheel slip and, most importantly, gives you something to think about other than how much you hate uphills.

DOWNHILL RIDING: Descending requires finesse and balance with the added element of control. Before beginning any significant descent, lower your center of gravity by lowering your seat post one to three inches. Shift the chain to the large front sprocket; this will prevent the chainwheel from engaging your leg should you become disengaged from the bike

5

(only practical for extended downhill runs; rapid transitions from down- to uphill require lower gearing and small sprockets). Pedals should be kept parallel to the ground with the front pedal riding slightly higher; this will prevent the pedals from catching the ground and causing an un- planned sprawl.

While cornering, pedal weight should be shifted to the outside, forcing that pedal down and the inside pedal up; this will help you corner and prevents snagging your inside pedal while keeping your weight centered over the bike. Be mindful of keeping your weight on the pedals instead of the seat; it is easier to shift weight when necessary. Hug the seat with your thighs and keep your knees flexed and ready to absorb terrain dif- ferences. Injuries occur most often when excessive speed causes a loss of control. In the beginning, try only a few of these techniques each time you ride, lest you spend more time thinking about what you should be doing and less about the fun you're having. Relax, or you won't feel a thing.

WATER CROSSING: Controlled momentum and keeping your weight over the seat will mean the difference between negotiating the water trap or taking a swim. It is possible to pedal steadily through up to a foot of water by avoiding large rocks, deep silt, and bad Karma.

USING YOUR BRAKES: The key to successful braking, especially when descending, is using your head. Remember that the amount of braking efficiency is directly proportional to the amount of weight (your weight) that each tire is carrying. On downhills your front wheel is carry- ing a majority of your weight and even more weight is transferred to your front wheel when braking. Translated, this means that your front wheel (front brake) is your "favorite pal" during downhill runs and is more likely to control your descent without going into the dreaded "locked wheel, no-control skid." This is not to say forget your rear brake. Good riders learn to apply just as much brake pressure as is necessary for the terrain. Only practice will allow you to judge how much front and rear brake you need to provide control and avoid jackknifes, rear-wheel skids, and front- wheel lockup.

Your body positioning is also important here. Ideal positioning pushes your fanny out over your rear wheel with your thighs gripping your seat. Experiment and discover what feels most comfortable to you. The more you shift your weight back over your rear wheel during downhills, the more you increase your rear wheel's braking power. Conversely, the more you shift your weight forward, the more you unweight your rear wheel and the greater the opportunity you have to demonstrate a swan dive over your handlebars — not a pretty sight. The lesson here is to keep your weight as far back as possible. On level ground an equal use of front and rear brake is appropriate because both of your wheels are equally weighted.

In summary then: the wheel with the most weight holds the greatest braking power; on downhills, shift your weight to the rear and learn to use firm pressure on your front brake with your rear brake as support; never lock up your rear wheel on downhills.

TURNING AND DIRECTIONAL CONTROL: First tip, avoid oversteering at all costs. Second tip, relax. Many beginners and even experienced riders lock their arms and resort to the "death grip" while descending, especially when loose soil or ruts are involved. Learn to use your body and not your arms to determine direction. Keep a firm, but relaxed grip on your handlebars and initiate turns by slightly twisting your shoulders into them. As you twist your shoulders, your bike will follow (skiers will recognize this technique as similar to squaring their shoulders into the fall line).

MISCELLANEOUS RIDING TIPS: Tire pressure is an important ingredient to successful traction and ease of pedaling. We recommend, depending on the tire type, soft tires (between 25 and 40 psi, not mushy, but soft to the squeeze of thumb and forefingers) for sandy and loose terrain. For firm terrain and hard ground, again depending on the tire type, higher pressure is the norm (between 35 and 50 psi, resistant to squeezing between thumb and forefinger, but not rock hard). Use caution when riding on soft tires; you are more likely to damage your rim and become the victim of pinched-tire flats.

Pedaling through deep sand is exhausting and technically difficult. This is one of those situations when your bike knows best. Relax and let the bike somewhat steer itself. Hold your momentum upon approach and entry. Downshift as low as is necessary without expending too much energy. During downhill runs learn to "bunny hop" your front wheel over ruts, washouts, potholes, and other small unavoidable obstacles.

For energy conservation, use "revolutionary pedaling" when possible. While pushing down with one pedal, use your toe clips to pull up the other pedal. This offers you increased power and efficiency.

Keep your bike clean after rides. Accumulated dust and grit on the chain, cables, and gears encourages increased wear and tear and untimely equipment failure.

STRETCHING: The majority of biking injuries can be alleviated by stretching muscles before and after riding. Jumping onto your bike without a warm-up is very hard on your body, regardless of physical condition. Besides, a general five-to-ten-minute stretching program will also do wonders for your riding ability. Pay particularly close attention to stretching thigh and calf muscles; lower, middle, and upper back muscles; and neck muscles. Think of the minutes spent as insurance against months of recuperation caused by injury.

### Keeping Your Bike Clean

Winter riding around the Bay Area brings to mind two things. First, if you are thinking of riding your bike on muddy trails, don't! You'll only churn up the mud and ruin the trail. Second, no matter where you ride, dirty, wet, and/or sandy conditions dictate that you clean your bike frequently. Grit and sand act as a grinding agent, wearing down every moving part in your bike. The sooner you remove the grime the longer the life of your bike and its various parts.

Use the following as a guide to degritting your bike:

1. RINSE: Remove caked-on mud, gunk, and grime by gently spraying with a garden hose. Never use high pressure; it is possible to blast water into the sealed bearings of the hubs and crank. Also, don't ever wipe dirt or mud from your frame with a rag as you risk scratching and ruining the finish.

2. DEGREASE: Remove the wheels and set them aside. Using a bucket of warm water and a mild detergent, scrub the derailleurs, chain, and chainrings with a bottle brush. Rinse, using the bottle brush again to scrub the chain, derailleurs, and chainring. You may need a small knife or screwdriver to help pry stubborn crud out of the chainwheel.

3. WASH: Using a floor-type bristle brush, warm water, and a mild detergent gently wash the frame and wheels. A bottle brush is useful for getting behind the chainrings and other such hard to reach spots. Next, start at the hubs and work out cleaning both wheels. Scrub the rim and tires with a floor brush to remove oil and tar residue.

4. FINAL RINSE: Reinstall the wheels and gently rinse off the entire bike. Once again, be careful not to blast water into the bearings.

5. DRY THOROUGHLY: Wipe off surface water with a soft towel. Put your bike in a warm place to dry. The tubes of your bike should have drain holes to help let the moisture out. Hanging your bike by its front wheel and removing the seat will allow some moisture that may have collected in the frame tubes to drain out the seat tube.

### Lubrication

Once your bike is dry, you will need to lubricate the parts that you degreased and any other areas that may need attention.

1. CHAIN, DERAILLEUR PULLEYS: For dry weather, use a lube that will penetrate, such as Tri-Flow. Be careful not to overspray on the rims and always wipe away excess lubrication. For wet or muddy terrain use a heavy oil like Campagnolo or Phil Wood. It does collect dirt, but the heavy oil displaces the mud and prevents anything nasty from penetrating into your chain or derailleur.

2. CABLES: While some manufacturers recommend running the cables

dry, performance in very wet conditions may be improved with application of silicone to the cable end buttons and entrance points — check with your bike shop for advice.

3. SEALED BEARINGS: Unless you are a mechanic, it is best to have your favorite bike shop do this for you periodically. It involves removing a seal, flushing out the old grease with solvent, drying thoroughly, and then repacking with new grease.

4. SEAT POST: Keep this clean and lightly greased with a heavy grease like Campagnolo.

5. SADDLE: Preserve leather by rubbing with Brooks Proofhide and then lightly dusting with talc.

6. PUMP: Keep leather gaskets lubricated with Vaseline and rubber gaskets with K-Y jelly.

### Creative Tire Repair

"Hissssssssssss, thwipitty, thwipitty, thwipitty" — it's a sound any mountain biker (or road biker) hates to hear. It means the ride has temporarily been interrupted for a tire-repair session. Some repairs are simple: a little glue, a small patch, a few hundred mantras while pumping, and, presto, the tire is good as new. There there are those few times, however, when the repair may appear hopeless — like when you are gazing at the spot on your bike frame where the pump is supposed to be but isn't.

Since you can't ride on a flat tire without ruining the rim, you need something to fill the tire with other than air — no pump, no air. By carefully stuffing the tire with grass, leaves, paper (anything that is not sharp), you will be able to ride out slowly. Your tire will still be very soft, so avoid rocks and large bumps, but you will be able to ride and that sure beats walking.

Those who ride a lot will know to carry an extra tube for those times when a patch just isn't enough. But, even then, bad Karma has a way of creeping up in bunches. When the patches run out, you do have one alternative. Tie a knot in the inner tube before and after the leak. Insert the tube back in the tire and pump up. The ride will be a little uneven, but at least it's a ride.

A gash in the sidewall of a tire is a slightly different situation. With no retaining wall, the tube will begin to bulge out and before long, the tube will pop. When a gash appears, reach for a piece of cardboard, a strip of bark, part of a soda can, even Power Bar wrappers have been known to work. Position the patch, known in official lingo as a boot, inside the wall of the tire, making sure that the boot is twice the size of the offending gash. Inflate the inner tube slowly so the boot does not slip. Once you pump up to maximum pressure, the tube will hold the boot in place.

For a really serious and large gash, use a combination of several boots inside the tire and a secure wrapping of duct tape outside the tire. It may look funny, but the tape should last you long enough until you get home or to a shop to buy a new tire. Don't forget to check the boot or boots periodically while riding to make sure that they haven't shifted.

# Tour Format

For ease of use, each tour follows the same format. Pertinent information is presented first in capsule form. A full description follows. Before riding, become familiar with the tour by reading the trail description; this will lessen the chances of missing an important turn or, worse, spending the day with your eyes on the guide instead of enjoying your surroundings.

TOPO: This refers to the USGS topographic quadrangle by name and size; whenever possible, all maps are 7.5′ for best detail. These are usually available from backpacking or mountaineering shops. We are lucky to have a local USGS office in Menlo Park at 345 Middlefield Road (415-853-8300); it usually has the best stock. Although we include a map for all tours, these are only for rough orientation and are not a substitute for a topo map. Because of the long periods between USGS updates, trails are frequently not shown; look for major landmarks and cross-reference with the included trail maps.

TRAILHEAD: For consistency, this is the starting area where the tour actually begins — not always where you have parked your car.

OVERALL DIFFICULTY: A comprehensive evaluation of the tour that account for distance, elevation loss and gain, and technical difficulty. Riding a tour in the opposite direction from that described will often greatly increase the difficulty. The ratings are as follows: easy (mostly flat, with few hills — an hour or so of riding time), easy/moderate (increasing hills but still mostly flat of short distance — an hour or two of riding time), moderate (generally hilly terrain with some rough terrain and occasional obstacles — two to three hours of riding time), strenuous (long distances with rough terrain, long, steep ascents and descents and very rough terrain — three to four hours of riding time) and most strenuous (gonzo, better have a few double espressos before saddling up — ridiculously long, steep climbs and drops, and lots of obstacles). Note: The times listed are our times — yours may vary wildly; also, these times don't allow for breaks for refueling, philosophizing, contemplating your navel or general safety meetings.

11

TECHNICAL DIFFICULTY: Everything that makes a tour interesting! Includes severe ascents and descents, negotiating and/or avoiding stream crossings, sand, scree, rocks, boulders, ruts, water bars, gopher holes, fallen trees, and a few other surprises constructed by humans or nature. The following are the gradations for overall and technical difficulty: easy, easy/moderate, moderate, moderate/difficult, difficult, and most difficult (see above ratings for descriptions).

A Note on Ratings: Accurately rating a mountain biking tour is very difficult. A myriad of variables involving weather, trail conditions, and temperature may drastically affect the difficulty of the ride; add differing abilities to this formula and complete accuracy in rating becomes impossible (one person's leisurely cruise may be another's death ride from hell!). Therefore, use these rating as an overall comparison with other rides within the guide; if you've ridden a tour rated as moderate but experienced great difficulty, keep this in mind when selecting the next tour. Note that riding during times of wet weather will upgrade most rides one to two difficulty ratings—the easy ascent that we described may become epic in proportion; even flat rides can become nightmarish mud slogs (see Rules of the Trail).

DISTANCE: The approximate total round-trip distance. It may seem obvious in the comfort of your home, but remember to allow enough time, energy, and daylight to finish a ride. Often the first half of a ride is much easier than the final half, particularly after gorging on a well-deserved picnic lunch. We have tried to be as accurate as possible using a bike-mounted odometer, map-measuring wheel, and official park mileage information. However, nothing is guaranteed to the foot.

HIGHLIGHTS: The points of interest of an area, including the natural history, flora, and fauna. Although the Bay Area's recorded history is relatively recent, much of it is fascinating and colored by the entrepreneurs who were drawn to the area from around the world. Many of the rides pass through their realm; close your eyes and you may hear their ghosts still going about their business.

GETTING THERE: Directions for driving from major landmarks and/or freeways to the parking area

THE RIDE: The detailed description of a tour. Usually noted are terrain transitions, intersections, stream crossings, forks, gates, and highlights of the trail. Although we have gone to lengths to assure accuracy, we are not infallible, and government policy on the use of mountain bikes is subject to change. Most areas described in this guide have a visitor's center. Inquire here about trail conditions and bicycle access; if this isn't available, look for an information board, which is usually near the trailhead. Remember that trails are closed for good reason—please abide by the rules.

TRAIL MAP: An outline of the trail description with parking, trailheads, mileage markers, and major landmarks. Maps are hand drawn from other published maps of varying scale and are only for general reference to aid in understanding the descriptions. For those exploring the more remote and advanced trails, we recommend using the trail maps in conjunction with USGS topographic maps. Some of the maps may cover more than one tour; each tour is noted with a number that corresponds to the ride and an arrow dictating the direction of travel.

ELEVATION GRAPH: An illustration of a trail's ascents and descents (perhaps too much so!) using the gradient as a graph. Mileage is shown horizontally; elevation in feet is illustrated vertically. Included are major landmarks that correspond with the trail map. Some long rides span several pages.

# Chapter One

# SAN ANDREAS AND SAWYER CAMP TRAILS

**TRAILHEAD:** *Crystal Springs Road and Skyline Boulevard*
**TOPO:** *San Mateo 7.5' and Montara Mountain 7.5'*
**OVERALL DIFFICULTY:** *Easy*
**TECHNICAL DIFFICULTY:** *Easy*
**DISTANCE:** *16.5 miles*

### Description

Located in San Mateo County alongside San Andreas Lake and Lower Crystal Springs Reservoir, San Andreas and Sawyer Camp trails are two of the most popular trails in the midcounty trail system. The valley through which these two trails run is known as the San Andreas Valley. This valley has been formed over the years partly by sinking of land within the San Andreas Fault zone and partly by stream erosion in the "crush" zone of the fault.

This particular area is very rich in anthropological and human history. Home for many thousands of years to the Shoshone, this land also became a stopping point for Gaspar de Portolá and his men in 1769. In 1774 Captain Rivera, an officer in Portolá's party, further explored the peninsula, camping near what is now know as Jepson Laurel. Jepson Laurel is one of the most famous landmarks on the Sawyer Camp Trail and, at over six hundred years of age, is the oldest and largest laurel in California.

The land, bought in later years by Leander Sawyer, was used for grazing cattle. The trail running through here was once the main highway from San Francisco to Half Moon Bay. When the City of San Francisco took over the land around 1888, it fenced in the road to protect San Francisco's drinking water. In 1978 San Mateo County designated the road a

15

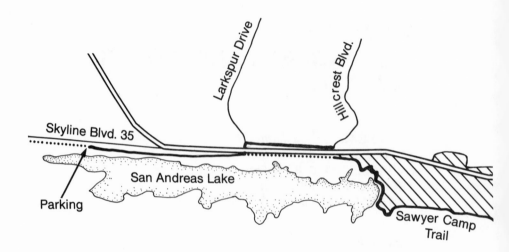

# SAN ANDREAS
# AND SAWYER CAMP TRAILS

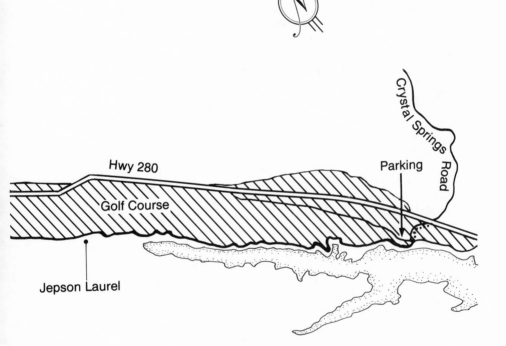

recreational trail and paved it for bicycles with money from the State Department of Parks and Recreation.

### Getting There

From Daly City and farther north, park at the northernmost point of the San Andreas Trail. From Highway 280 north take Skyline Boulevard exit to a point approximately .25 mile south of San Bruno Avenue. Parking is at the signed trail entrance on the west side of the road. From 280 south take Sneath Lane and go south on the frontage road to San Bruno Avenue. Turn right on San Bruno Avenue to Skyline Boulevard, where you will turn left and drive about .25 mile to the parking area.

From the south, park at the southernmost point for Sawyer Camp Trail. From 280 north, exit Bunker Hill Road and turn left to Skyline Boulevard. Turn right on Skyline and drive north .5 mile to Crystal Springs Road. Parking is along Skyline Boulevard just past the trail entrance.

### The Ride

Whether you start at the north and ride south, or start at the south and ride north, the ride is an easy and enjoyable out-and-back journey for all levels. It is perhaps a little easier to begin the ride from the south because the 400 feet of elevation gain is gradually accomplished in the beginning and the ride is all downhill or level from then on. (*NOTE: Bicycles are restricted to the paved surface only on Sawyer Camp Trail.*)

Beginning at the Crystal Springs entrance, ride north on the paved Sawyer Camp Trail. At 3.5 miles the trail passes the Jepson Laurel, named after Willis Jepson, noted 1920s California botanist. At 4.7 miles the trail will begin to climb gradually to San Andreas Lake and Dam and then up to Skyline Boulevard. If you wish to cut your ride short, you can turn around here and your round-trip mileage will be 12 miles.

If you wish to continue on, you will need to ride about .8 mile of the east frontage road between Hillcrest Boulevard and Larkspur Drive. The present section of connecting trail between San Andreas Trail and Sawyer Camp Trail is not open to bicycles. Cross under Highway 280 on Hillcrest and turn left on Skyline Boulevard. Turn left on Larkspur Drive and join the San Andreas Trail "already in progress." Pedal another 1.5 miles to the trail end and turn around for the return trip back to your car. Although the freeway is very close on this last section, the views of the surrounding landscape and the proximity of a sparkling lake make this a most enjoyable addition.

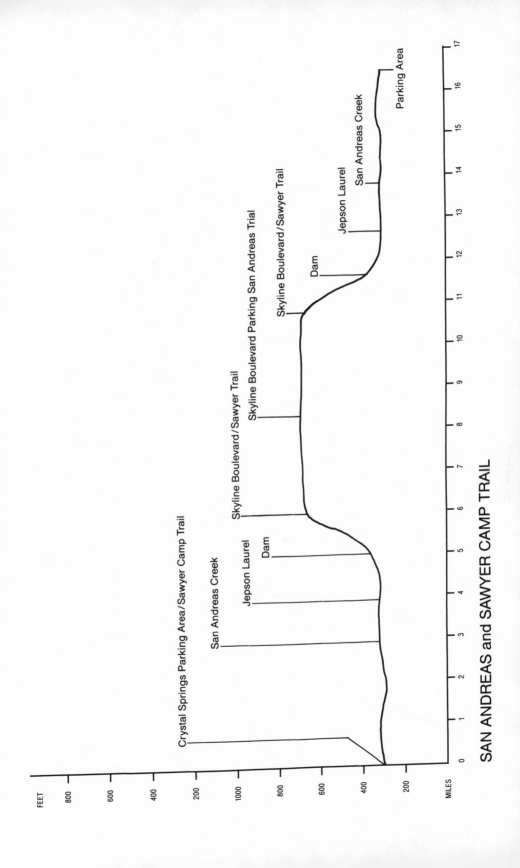

SAN ANDREAS and SAWYER CAMP TRAIL

## Chapter Two
# PORTOLA STATE PARK

**TRAILHEAD:** *Portola State Park*
**TOPO:** *La Honda 7.5' and Mindego Hill 7.5'*
**OVERALL DIFFICULTY:** *Easy/Moderate*
**TECHNICAL DIFFICULTY:** *Easy*
**DISTANCE:** *12.7 miles*

### Description

Portola State Park is a 2,400-acre evergreen forest set in the rugged land-scape of the northwestern Santa Cruz Mountains. The park is named after the Spanish explorer Don Gasper de Portolá, who led an expedition in 1769 through the area in search of anchorage for his boats. Later, because of the incredible demand for timber during and after the California Gold Rush, the Portola area was subjected to heavy logging in the late 1800s. It wasn't until 1945 that the State of California acquired 1,600 acres for use as a park. The additional 800 acres of land were donated by the Save-the-Redwoods League during subsequent years.

In addition to the Portola acreage, the development of an adjoining 7,000-plus acres of Pescadero Creek County Park allows the visitor a unique experience among the towering coastal redwoods and Douglas firs. Rushing streams, dense ferns, and open meadows provide the backdrop for this magnificent forest.

### Getting There

Portola State Park is located just a few miles southeast of La Honda in the Santa Cruz Mountains. One of the easiest ways to get to Portola is south on Alpine Road off Highway 35. To get there from San Jose take Highway 9; from Palo Alto take Page Mill Road; from Redwood City and

To La Honda

Pescadero Road

To Highway
1

Memorial Park

PESCADERO
COUNTY PARK

Old Haul Road

Butano Ridge Loop Trail

PORTOLA STATE PARK

□ County Jail

# PORTOLA STATE PARK

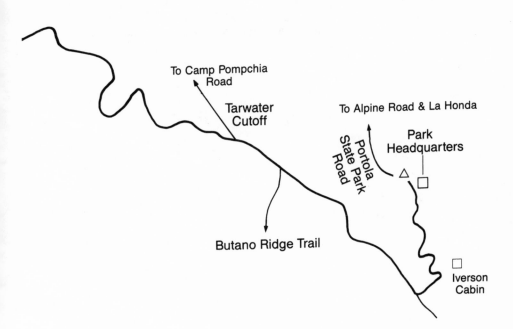

To Camp Pompchia Road

Tarwater Cutoff

To Alpine Road & La Honda

Portola State Park Road

Park Headquarters

Butano Ridge Trail

Iverson Cabin

points north take Highway 84. Once on Alpine Road you will drive approximately 3 miles to the turnoff onto Portola State Park Road. Be careful here as the next 4 miles to the parking area and park headquarters are a very narrow and winding descent. Park your car and begin your ride.

### The Ride

This ride is extremely well suited for all levels of mountain bikers. Beginning at the park headquarters, pedal down the road, cross the bridge and bear right at the junction toward the group picnic shelter, approximately .25 mile. Go through the service road gate and continue another .75 mile to Iverson Cabin and the park employee residences. Service vehicles occasionally use the road to this point, so be very careful and ready to yield at any time. Continue from Iverson Cabin about 200 yards to the gate and boundary with Pescadero Creek County Park. At the gate you will turn right onto Old Haul Road for a rolling but moderate ride to Memorial County Park and Pescadero Road. Once you reach Old Haul Road Trailhead and parking area, turn around and pedal back the way you came.

You will have every bit as much fun going back as you did getting here. The road is wide enough and moderate enough that a little speed offers minimal risks and maximum fun. As always, yield to hikers and equestrians. Round trip from the gate at Portola onto Old Haul Road and back is approximately 10 miles. Your total mileage round trip back to the parking area is approximately 12.7 miles. Starting elevation is 400 feet, climbing to 800 feet midway to Memorial Park and descending back to 400 feet. Have fun!

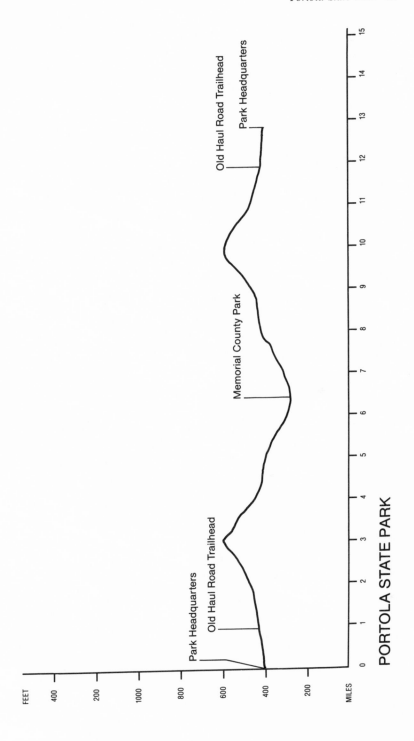

PORTOLA STATE PARK

## Chapter Three
# BUTANO STATE PARK

**TRAILHEAD:** *Park entrance gate on Cloverdale Road*
**TOPO:** *Franklin Point*

**RIDE #1** *(Park ranger escort only)*
**OVERALL DIFFICULTY:** *Easy*
**TECHNICAL DIFFICULTY:** *Easy/Moderate*
**DISTANCE:** *11.5 miles*

**RIDE #2**
**OVERALL DIFFICULTY:** *Moderate/Strenuous*
**TECHNICAL DIFFICULTY:** *Easy*
**DISTANCE:** *13 miles*

### *Highlights*

Nestled in the Santa Cruz Mountains of southern San Mateo County lies Butano State Park, a 2,200-acre redwood preserve. In the language of the Ohlones, Butano means roughly "gathering place of friendly people." This park is named because the area was the spring and summer commerce and social gathering center of the Ohlones. Logging the coastal redwood for shingles was big industry in this valley in the mid-1800s. The operation threatened to eliminate virtually all of the virgin redwood until, through a series of fluke circumstances, the logging mill's final owner committed suicide and all logging ceased. Little Butano Valley was saved, and one can now view excellent examples of coastal redwood. Although the area was considered for purchase as a park in the 1950s, it wasn't until 1961 that the park was finally dedicated.

Sandy hills and severe altitude gains make the self-guided rides in Butano

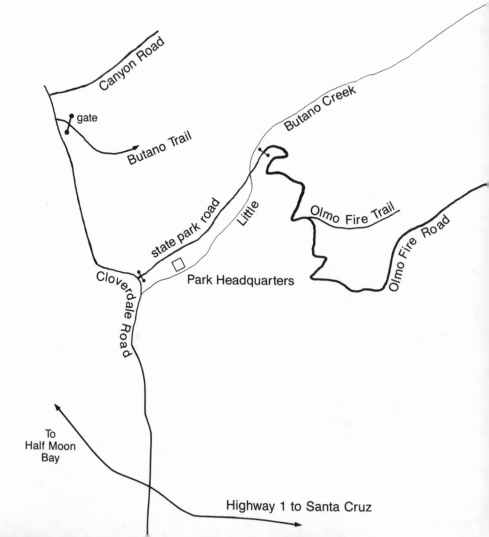

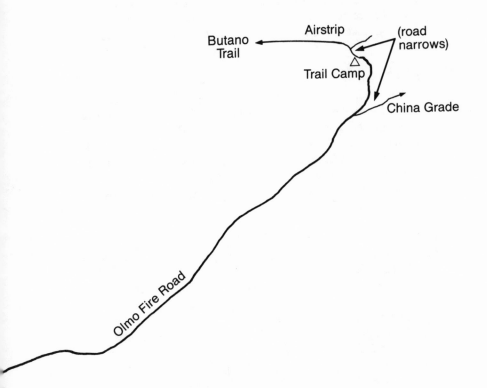

Airstrip

Butano
Trail

(road
narrows)

△
Trail Camp

China Grade

Olmo Fire Road

# BUTANO STATE PARK

suitable only for intermediates and above. If you consider yourself a hardy beginner, the scenic beauty is well worth the effort, although you may find that your bike wants to be walked a lot. Relax and let your heaving lungs recover.

### Getting There

Located between Half Moon Bay and Santa Cruz off Highway 1. Coming from Half Moon Bay, drive 14 miles from the last stop light on Highway 1 to Pescadero Road. Turn left and continue 2.25 miles to Cloverdale Road and turn right. Drive 5.5 miles to the park entrance on the left side. Coming from Santa Cruz, drive approximately 25 miles north on Highway 1 to Cloverdale Road, where you turn right. Continue 3 miles to the signed park entrance on your right. Parking may be found either at the entrance gate or at the picnic area.

### Ride #1

Perhaps the most scenic and certainly most gentle ride can only be done with a park ranger as guide. Riders of all levels will enjoy and appreciate this unique park-sponsored mountain bike ride. Ranger Michael McCabe designed this combination mountain bike ride and park interpretive program to promote responsible use of park lands and allow access into beautiful, but previously inaccessible, private holdings. The rides are held on weekends during the summer months only, and space must be reserved in advance at 415-879-0173 due to the popularity.

The ride winds gradually uphill for approximately 5.5 miles through dense stands of redwoods and Douglas fir, affording spectacular views (weather permitting) of the surrounding mountains and ocean. At the midsection the ride is mostly level for approximately 1 mile to allow time to get ready for the final 5-mile rapid descent. In addition to abundant wildlife, the periodic natural and anthropological information shared by the ranger/guide makes this a don't-miss opportunity. Please remember, since this particular ride crosses private land, it is only allowed when accompanied by a ranger.

### Ride #2

While this ride can certainly be enjoyed as a day trip, we are recommending it as an overnight possibility. The midway or turnaround point, Butano Trail Camp, is 6.5 miles from the park entrance and approximately 1,200 feet of elevation gain. Butano Trail Camp is a primitive trail camp with six sites that must be reserved in advance. Each site has space for a tent. No fires are allowed, there is a pit toilet, and you must bring in your own water at the present time.

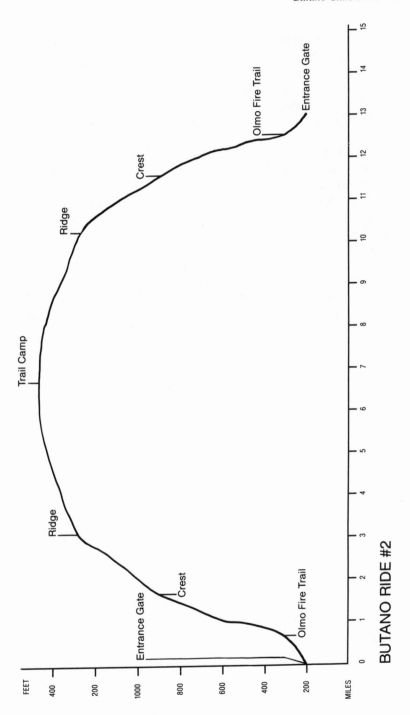

BUTANO RIDE #2

Beginning at the entrance gate, pedal approximately .5 mile on fairly level, paved road to the service gate for Olmo Fire Trail, where you turn right. The road turns rough and eventually to gravel as it winds its way steeply upward gaining 720 feet in just over a mile. Shortly after gaining relatively level ground you will notice a fire road branching off to the right. Turn right on the Olmo Fire Road, gaining another 400 feet of elevation over the next mile. As the trail opens up onto a sandy ridge you may wish to dismount and walk your bike — the next mile gains 500 very sandy feet. Take your time, enjoy the view and the small consolation that the return trip is much more fun.

As the ridge trail disappears back into the woods, and firmer ground, keep a sharp eye out for a left turn to the Butano Trail Camp. The access from Olmo Fire Road is narrow, like single track, so watch your speed. Once camp is set up, it is worth a short pedal .75 mile up the Butano Fire Trail to an old landing strip and excellent vistas. Do not proceed any farther than the landing strip with your mountain bike, as you will be trespassing on private land. The return trip is an "E ticket" ride back the way you came to the entrance gate and your car. Please watch your speed — others use the trail too.

## Chapter Four
# BIG BASIN STATE PARK

**TRAILHEAD:** *Big Basin Headquarters Rides #1 and #2; Waddell Beach*
  *Ride #3*
**TOPO:** *Big Basin 7.5'; Año Nuevo 7.5'; Franklin Point 7.5'*

*Ride #1*
**OVERALL DIFFICULTY:** *Strenuous*
**TECHNICAL DIFFICULTY:** *Difficult*
**DISTANCE:** *16.5 miles*

*Ride #2*
**OVERALL DIFFICULTY:** *Moderate/Strenuous*
**TECHNICAL DIFFICULTY:** *Moderate*
**DISTANCE:** *19.5 miles to bus or 13.5 miles with car shuttle*

*Ride #3*
**OVERALL DIFFICULTY:** *Easy/Moderate*
**TECHNICAL DIFFICULTY:** *Easy*
**DISTANCE:** *10.4 miles*

*Description*
Located in Santa Cruz County, Big Basin Redwoods State Park encompasses over 18,000 acres of some of the world's most beautiful and majestic redwoods. These trees have witnessed more than 1,000 years of man's transition: Ohlones passing through in reverence and awe, the Portolá expedition of 1769 camping at Waddell Creek, the lumber mills of 1862, and Big Basin's inception as a park in 1902.

At present the park boasts more than 100 miles of hiking trails, 183

33

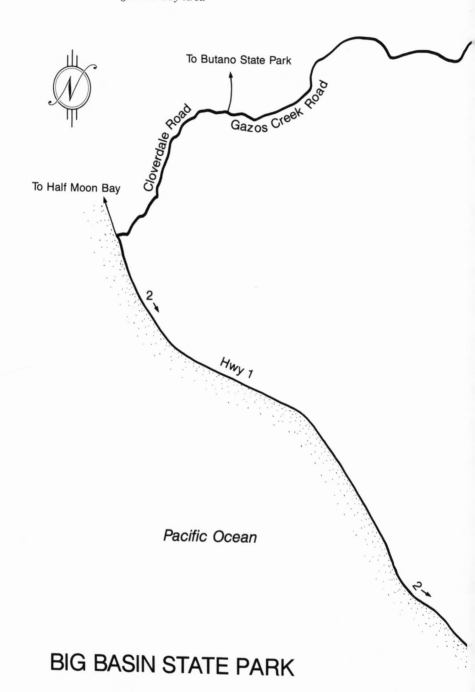

BIG BASIN STATE PARK

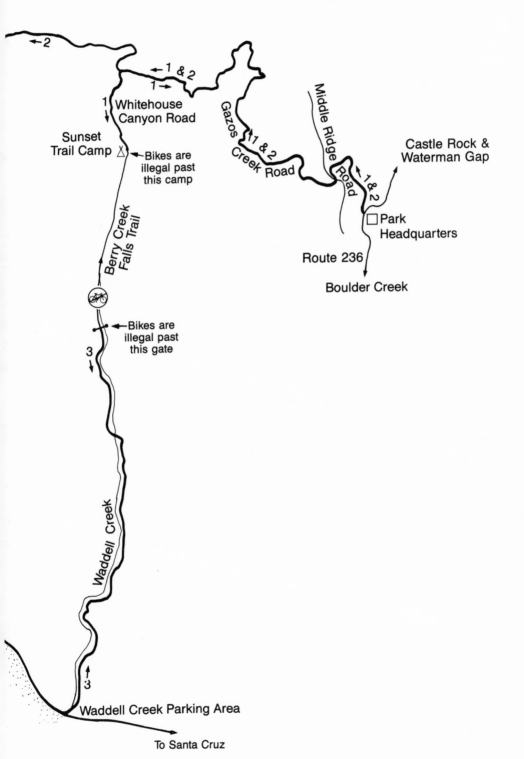

campsites, a nature center, and a combination camp store, gift shop, and snack bar. Although all of the single-track trails are closed to mountain bikes, there are still miles of service road and fire road to be explored. Bring your sense of wonder and adventure and enjoy this park to the fullest.

### Getting There

From Highway 9 and Boulder Creek, just north of Santa Cruz, drive 9 miles north on Highway 236. From Highway 9 off Highway 35 coming from Palo Alto or points north, drive approximately 8 miles south on Highway 236. Leave your vehicle at the park entrance/headquarter day-use parking area.

### The Ride

Big Basin offers numerous fire roads for mountain bike exploration. Check at the park headquarters for current trail status. We have selected three rides. One is an overnighter for strong riders; one a shuttle or bus trip to the coast, also for strong riders; the last an excellent out-and-back streamside pedal for any level. These rides provide a broad representation of the park's offerings. We do, however, encourage legal exploration on your own. Check with the park headquarters for other options.

### Ride #1

Beginning at the park headquarters and 1,000-foot elevation, ride approximately .5 mile north on the North Escape Road (Picnic Area Road) to the Gazos Creek Road turnoff. Bear left to the gate and continue 1.3 miles on easy terrain gaining 320 feet to the intersection with Middle Ridge Road. Continue on Gazos Creek Road, losing approximately 500 feet in 2 miles. The descent is easy and fun, but sharp and blind corners require controlled speed. Near the end of the downhill there is a gate — another reason to remain in control. Beyond the gate the riding becomes somewhat difficult due to very silty conditions combined with a steady climb. After 3 miles of this challenging terrain, Whitehouse Canyon will be encountered (6.5 miles from headquarters and elevation 1,350 feet); bear left and pedal a fairly level .5 mile to another gate and the turnoff for Sunset Trail Camp. The ride drops quickly, losing 350 feet in just under a mile. The road is rutted, so watch your speed. There are 10 sites here, all primitive and requiring reservations (call 408-338-6132). Camp stoves are required and you must provide your own water. Pit toilets are provided. Retrace your path to your car and the park headquarters for a total round-trip mileage of approximately 16.5 miles.

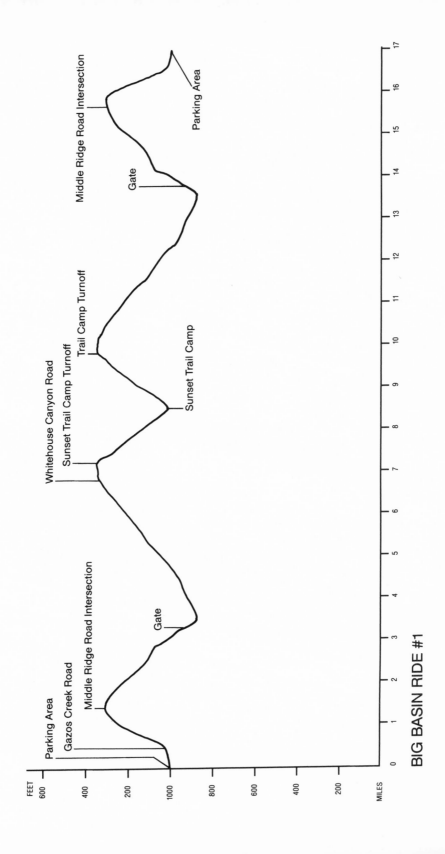

BIG BASIN RIDE #1

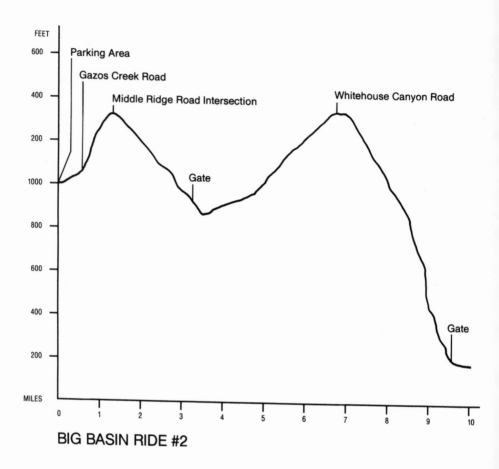

BIG BASIN RIDE #2

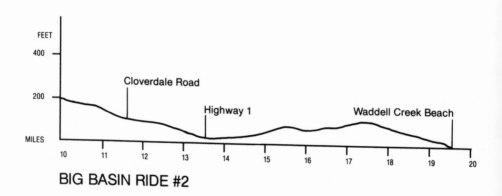

BIG BASIN RIDE #2

### Ride #2

This ride involves a car shuttle. You will need to leave one car at the intersection of Gazos Creek Road and Cloverdale Road. There is a small dirt parking area available.

This trip begins at the Big Basin Park Headquarters and follows Ride #1's description until Whitehouse Canyon Road. From the Whitehouse Canyon Road turnoff, continue straight on Gazos Creek Road. It is all downhill from here, 5 miles of downhill to be exact. The road is rough and used by logging trucks, so ride with caution. At about mile 3 during the descent, and approximately 200 feet elevation, you will encounter a gate over which you will have to lift your bike. The remaining 2 miles are relatively flat leading out to Cloverdale Road and your car.

### Ride #3

This ride begins and ends at the Waddell Beach Parking Area just off Highway 1 north of Santa Cruz and is perfect for all levels of riders. The ride is extremely scenic. Should you wish to turn this into an overnight, there are a number of trail camps along the way that are open to bicycles (contact Big Basin for reservations at 408-338-6132). From the parking area, pedal approximately 5.2 miles of relatively smooth and level dirt road to the trailhead for Berry Creek Falls.

This is as far as you can and will want to go with your bike; the falls, however, are well worth the visit. If you have a lock, leave your bike and hike to the falls, 2 miles round trip. Return the way you came. There is one stream crossing that gives you an option of using the bridge or crashing through the stream. If you are feeling adventurous and want to try your skills at stream crossing, downshift and go for it. Remember to keep your momentum going at a steady pace and keep your weight over your pedals. Wahoo!

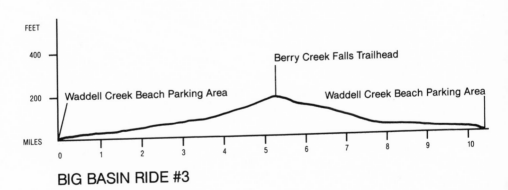

BIG BASIN RIDE #3

## Chapter Five
# WILDER RANCH STATE PARK

**TRAILHEAD:** *Wilder Ranch Complex (Cultural Preserve)*

*Ride #1*
**TOPO:** *Santa Cruz*
**OVERALL DIFFICULTY:** *Moderate*
**TECHNICAL DIFFICULTY:** *Easy*
**DISTANCE:** *5.9 miles*

*Ride #2*
**TOPO:** *Santa Cruz; Felton*
**OVERALL DIFFICULTY:** *Moderate*
**TECHNICAL DIFFICULTY:** *Difficult*
**DISTANCE:** *12 miles*

*Ride #3*
**TOPO:** *Santa Cruz*
**OVERALL DIFFICULTY:** *Moderate/Difficult*
**TECHNICAL DIFFICULTY:** *Difficult*
**DISTANCE:** *4.5 miles*

*Highlights*
Simply put, we consider this to be the premier park in the Bay Area. Wilder has it all: meandering fire roads, challenging climbs, technical single track, stunning beauty, wildlife, redwoods, incredible views and an interesting history to boot.

The present park stands on what was once Rancho del Matadero, started by Mission Santa Cruz in 1791. The preserve contains Native American

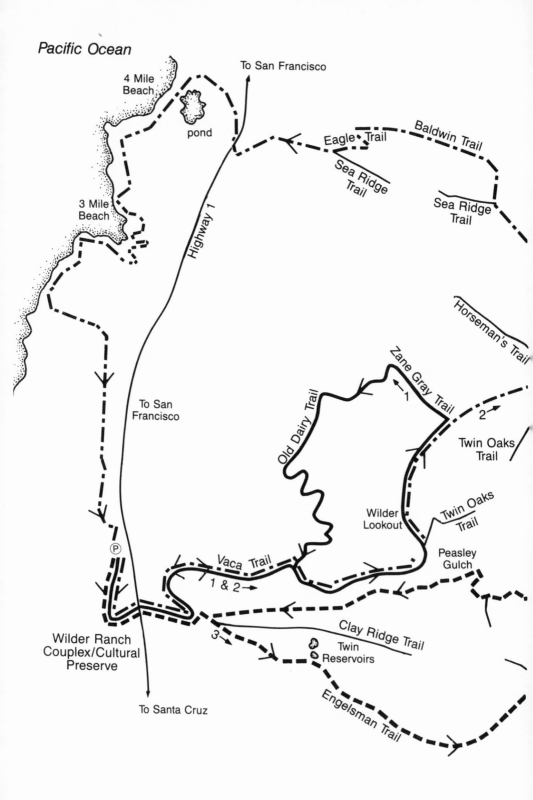

# WILDER RANCH STATE PARK
# RIDES #1, #2, and #3

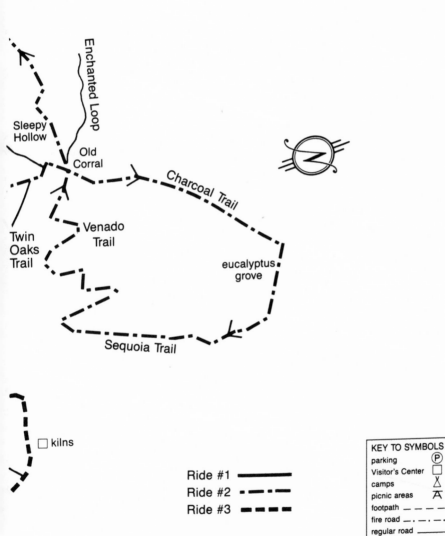

Enchanted Loop

Sleepy
Hollow

Old
Corral

Charcoal Trail

Venado
Trail

Twin
Oaks
Trail

eucalyptus
grove

Sequoia Trail

kilns

Ride #1
Ride #2
Ride #3

KEY TO SYMBOLS
parking               P
Visitor's Center
camps
picnic areas
footpath _ _ _ _
fire road _._._.
regular road _____
designated trail ▬▬▬

village sites, a Mexican-era adobe, and 19th- and 20th-century ranch buildings. Much of the area has been restored to reflect its historic use as a dairy, complete with animals, gardens and workshops.

On weekends many demonstrations are given, including blacksmithing, butter making and old-fashioned games. The large band saw on the near the Victorian is the original tool used to cut most of the timbers for the Wilder Ranch; look closely and you'll see that it's waterpowered (by a Pelton Water Wheel to be exact) and still operational. Anyone interested in California history will enjoy viewing the demonstrations.

Yet Wilder is a recently opened park in danger of closing because of budgetary constraints. Please help us to maintain this park by paying the state park entry fees and strictly following all guidelines; those feeling even more inclined can make donations to the Friends of Wilder Association. Information is available at the visitor's center.

### Getting There
The entrance to Wilder Ranch is located on Highway 1 just north of Santa Cruz. From Santa Cruz take Highway 1 north 1.8 miles from Western Drive (the last stoplight when leaving town) and turn left (west); follow the paved road .8 mile past fields of Brussels sprouts to the state park kiosk and parking area.

### Ride #1
Beginning at the parking area, ride west down a short paved hill (control your speed as there are pedestrians in this area) and turn left (north) into the Wilder Ranch Complex and Cultural Preserve and dismount—maps are available in the visitor's center. Cyclists are requested to walk their bikes through this area as there are often young children about. Walking also provides visitors the chance to enjoy some of the park's history. If you're lucky there may be a tortilla-making demonstration back by the old adobe—a great opportunity for some last-minute carbo loading!

After passing through the Complex, remount and pedal through the tunnel/Highway 1 overpass and over a cattle guard; continue on the dirt road (Vaca Trail) .5 mile to its intersection with the Engelsman Trail (Ride #3 continues straight on this trail) and hook a nearly 180-degree turn to the left and continue on the Vaca Trail. Pedal up a short but somewhat steep incline. Looking ahead to the bluff (which may or may not be a great idea, depending upon how one is feeling at this point) is Wilder Overlook— a destination on our route. On the left is one of the reservoirs of the area—if your Karma is good and you're quiet enough, you may be able to spot the resident great blue heron doing some fishing in the reservoir.

Back to the task at hand: continue on the Vaca Trail over gently rolling terrain, past the intersection with the Old Dairy Trail at mile 1.4, staying to the right. Prepare to drop some gears and engage in some heavy breathing as the route ascends up Wilder Overlook. The first pitch ascends up and into a stand of bay laurel and alder trees before flattening out somewhat; on the right is the intersection with Twin Oaks Trail — continue on the trail to the left where it steepens again and ascends up the back side of the overlook. Once on the top continue straight out on the overlook for a very rewarding view of Santa Cruz, Monterey Bay, the Pacific Ocean, numerous beaches and the University of California Santa Cruz. Elevation at the overlook: 520 feet. Distance from the trailhead: 2.3 miles.

Follow the ridge for a short distance to the intersection with Zane Gray Trail at mile 2.8 (Ride #2 continues straight here) and turn left and descend down the somewhat steep sections — remember to keep speed under control and watch for equestrians and hikers. At the intersection with Old Dairy Trail stay left and the trail flattens and contours until it rejoins with Vaca Trail at mile 4.5; turn right and retrace path back to the Complex (remember to dismount when passing through) and the parking area at mile 5.9.

## Ride #2

This ride is one to showcase for out-of-town guests. It offers much in the way of history, challenging climbs, view of the bay, wildlife, exciting single track, stream crossings and finishes up with an easy pedal along the ocean cliffs — what more can you ask for? Moab, eat your heart out.

Follow description for Ride #1 to Wilder Ridge/Zane Gray Trail. At mile 2.8, continue straight on Wilder Ridge Trail over rolling terrain staying to the left past the intersection with Twin Oaks Trail; a very short distance and Horsemen's Trail will also be encountered — stay to the right on the gravel road until it once again becomes dirt and sand. The

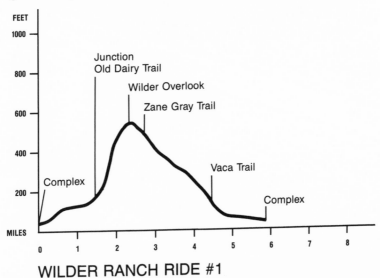

WILDER RANCH RIDE #1

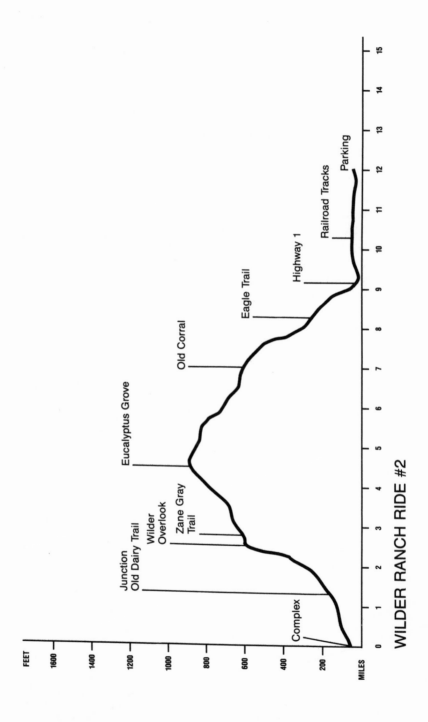

WILDER RANCH RIDE #2

route becomes somewhat confusing here; stay to the right (east) until an old corral is encountered at mile 3.5.

At this point, single-track Venado Trail (not to worry — you'll be returning on this trail) is to the right; continue straight on Charcoal Trail and begin climbing approximately 1 mile to elevation 840 feet to a eucalyptus grove. Use a bit of caution as you pass through this grove as more than a few spokes and derailleurs have been broken by the mischievous branches that reside here!

Prepare for a bit of nirvana for the next mile — downhill with few obstacles. Remember that others are also using the trail. I once encountered a coyote on this section — she paralleled me until she became bored and disappeared back into the brush — so please keep your speed under check. As the road enters the trees and becomes single track, gear down and be prepared for some interesting sections of single track and hair pins. Old mountain biking proverb: Remember to keep your nose over your toes. Also, ride low, you go; ride high, you die (well maybe not quite that bad).

After a mile of single-track bliss you will find yourself back at the old corral (sounds like a cowboy movie); retrace your path a very short distance to the confusing intersection of Enchanted Loop to the right and Wilder Ridge Trail to the left at mile 6.9; follow the route straight ahead on Sleepy Hollow through a beautiful stand of trees and up onto an open ridge line. Continue on mostly rolling terrain to the intersection with Rim Trail, stay right and continue on Baldwin Trail. From here the trail descends, steeply at times, over very broken terrain — mostly limestone rocks and stones; pick a line through this, keep your momentum but stay in control and avoid skidding.

At mile 8.4 turn left on single-track Eagle Trail (beware of stinging nettles in this area) and descend to a small drainage and and then ascend and cross a short section of limestone to the intersection with Sea Ridge Trail and turn right and parallel the fields (be sure not to disturb or ride through any of the fields in this area) to the intersection with Poppy Trail; keep to the left and descend down to a gate and Highway 1 at mile 9.0.

Head north on Highway 1 (use extreme caution here as traffic on this highway travels at very high speeds — stay well over on the shoulder) a very short distance (approximately .1 mile) and then cross the highway at the dirt parking area and follow a dirt road toward the ocean and Four Mile Beach.

Once at the beach, dismount (unless you're the type that enjoys riding this sort of terrain) and walk up toward the bluff to the east; route finding is slightly tricky through here, just follow the trail to the top of the bluff above the pond until a trail is encountered.

Follow this trail as it winds around the bluffs above beautiful Ohlone

Beach. Just past the beach, follow the dirt road up to the railroad tracks, turn right on the dirt road and parallel the tracks approximately 1.5 miles and cross at where the road intersects. Climb up a very short incline and follow the dirt road a short distance back to the parking area at mile 12.

### Ride #3

Follow the description for Ride #1 to the intersection of Vaca and Engelsman trails at mile .5; continue straight on Engelsman. A very short distance and another fork is encountered. To the far left is Wagon Wheel Trail; our route will be returning on this trail. The middle trail is Clay Ridge Trail. Follow the Engelsman Trail on the right and begin climbing. The next 1.5 miles climb 400 hundred feet, most of it within the first mile. Practice your Zen beingness and try not to think about your heaving chest, pounding heart and burning thighs.

At approximately mile 2 the trail flattens out somewhat and parallels the park boundaries. At the Wild Boar and Lime Kiln Trail intersection continue straight on Lime Kiln; to the north outside the park (please stay within boundaries) are the namesake kilns. At mile 2.6 the trail becomes single track and hooks to the left and enters the land of poison oak — beware of offending tendrils. At mile 3.4 an old, abandoned truck is encountered. The first creek crossing comes at mile 3.7, and there are several several crossings are ahead. The trail widens a short distance ahead, and at mile 4.2 it intersects with Clay Ridge and Engelsman. If you're looking for an additional workout, turn up Clay Ridge to its intersection with Wild Boar Trail — be prepared for some really wonderful kidney jarring! To return to the parking area, retrace your path the way you came.

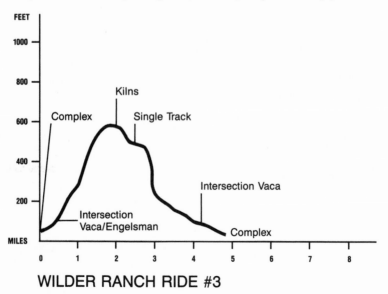

WILDER RANCH RIDE #3

## Chapter Six
# LONG RIDGE
# OPEN SPACE PRESERVE

**TRAILHEAD:** *Parking pullout off Skyline Boulevard for Long Ridge and Grizzly Flat*
**TOPO:** *Mindego Hill 7.5'*
**OVERALL DIFFICULTY:** *Easy/Moderate*
**TECHNICAL DIFFICULTY:** *Easy/Moderate*
**DISTANCE:** *7.6 miles*

### Description
Managed by the Midpeninsula Open Space District, Long Ridge Open Space Preserve is a wonderful playground for hikers, bikers, and equestrians. This preserve offers some excellent opportunities to enjoy legal single-track mountain biking. Dedicated to managing the balanced use of recreation and environmental protection, Long Ridge Open Space features much in the way of shaded forest, oak-studded meadows, winding trails, and magnificent views.

As you enjoy the area observe the tree stumps, abandoned orchards, and open grassland that may once have been used as hay fields by homesteaders in the late 1860s. Since you will be riding on single tract, watch your speed and control; others use the trails too. Be sure to pack a picnic lunch or take some time to pause on the open ridges overlooking the Santa Cruz Mountains—the views are spectacular.

### Getting There
Located on Highway 35 midway between Page Mill Road (to the north) and Saratoga Gap and Highway 9 (to the south). Parking is provided on

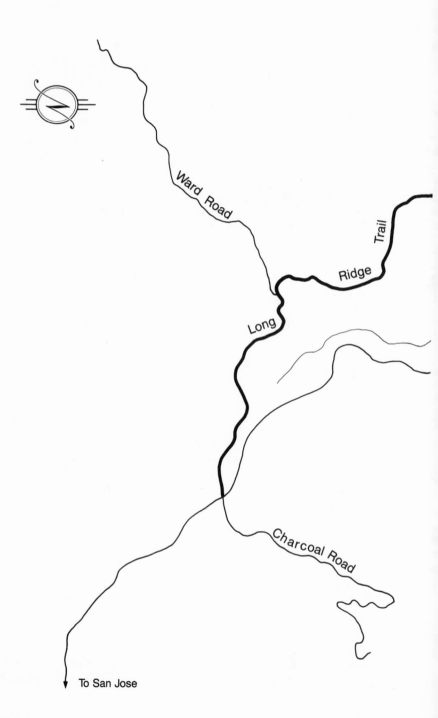

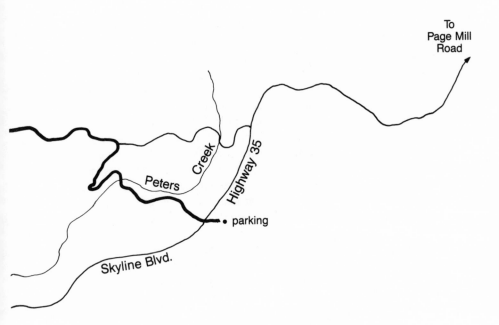

△ Table Mountain

# LONG RIDGE OPEN SPACE PRESERVE

either side of Highway 35 and the trailheads for Long Ridge Open Space and Grizzly Flat.

### The Ride

Round trip is approximately 7.6 miles and suitable for all levels of riders. Begin on the south side of Highway 35 and the trailhead for Long Ridge/ Peters Creek Trail. Descend .4 mile on single track with a few sharp turns to a stream crossing and the intersection of the Long Ridge and Peters Creek trails. Bear left and parallel along the stream toward the Long Ridge Trail. As the terrain opens into a meadow, stay alert. You will want to bear right and pedal up the ridge approximately 150 yards after entering the meadow.

From the meadow, the trail widens into a fire road and climbs gently to a hairpin turn and the intersection with Long Ridge Trail. It is approximately 1.3 miles from the trailhead to this point. Head left and up onto more single track. This single track will take you up another .9 mile of sharply winding trail to the ridge. Bear left on the fire road and pedal another .5 mile to the intersection of Long Ridge Trail and Ward Road.

Continue on Long Ridge another 1.1 rolling miles until you reach its intersection with Highway 35. Turn around and ride back the way you came. Keep in mind that this time you will be descending much of the single track you came up and that it is heavily used by hikers and other bikers; watch your speed and be courteous.

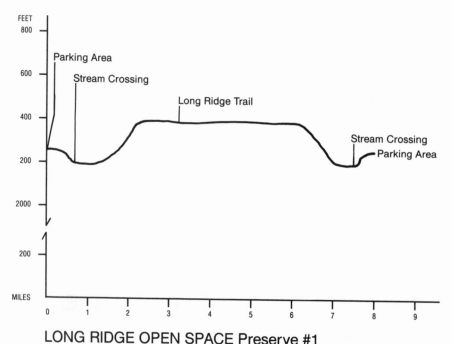

LONG RIDGE OPEN SPACE Preserve #1

**Chapter Seven**

# SARATOGA GAP—
# GRIZZLY FLAT LOOP

**TRAILHEAD:** *Saratoga Gap*
**TOPO:** *Mindego Hill 7.5' and Cupertino 7.5'*
**OVERALL DIFFICULTY:** *Moderate*
**TECHNICAL DIFFICULTY:** *Moderate*
**DISTANCE:** *Approximately 9.7 miles*

### Highlights
Long Ridge Open Space is known for its spectacular views of Big Basin State Park and Butano Ridge. Wide-open grasslands interspersed with oak, madrone, and fir woodlands typify the region. Saratoga Gap is primarily Douglas fir forest with small meadows and some grassy hills. Lichen-covered boulders and sandstone rock outcrops provide special scenic value as do Stevens Creek Canyon and the creek itself. Excellent picnic spots may be had alongside Stevens Creek adjacent to the Canyon Trail.

### Getting There
The parking area is located at the junction of Big Basin Way (State Highway 9) and Skyline Boulevard (Highway 35). From Saratoga, follow Highway 9 to the junction. Parking is to the left. The trailhead is immediately to the right of Highway 9 before turning left onto Skyline and entering the parking area.

### The Ride
From the parking area cross Highway 9 to the northeast corner of the intersection and the entrance for Saratoga Gap Open Space Preserve. The

53

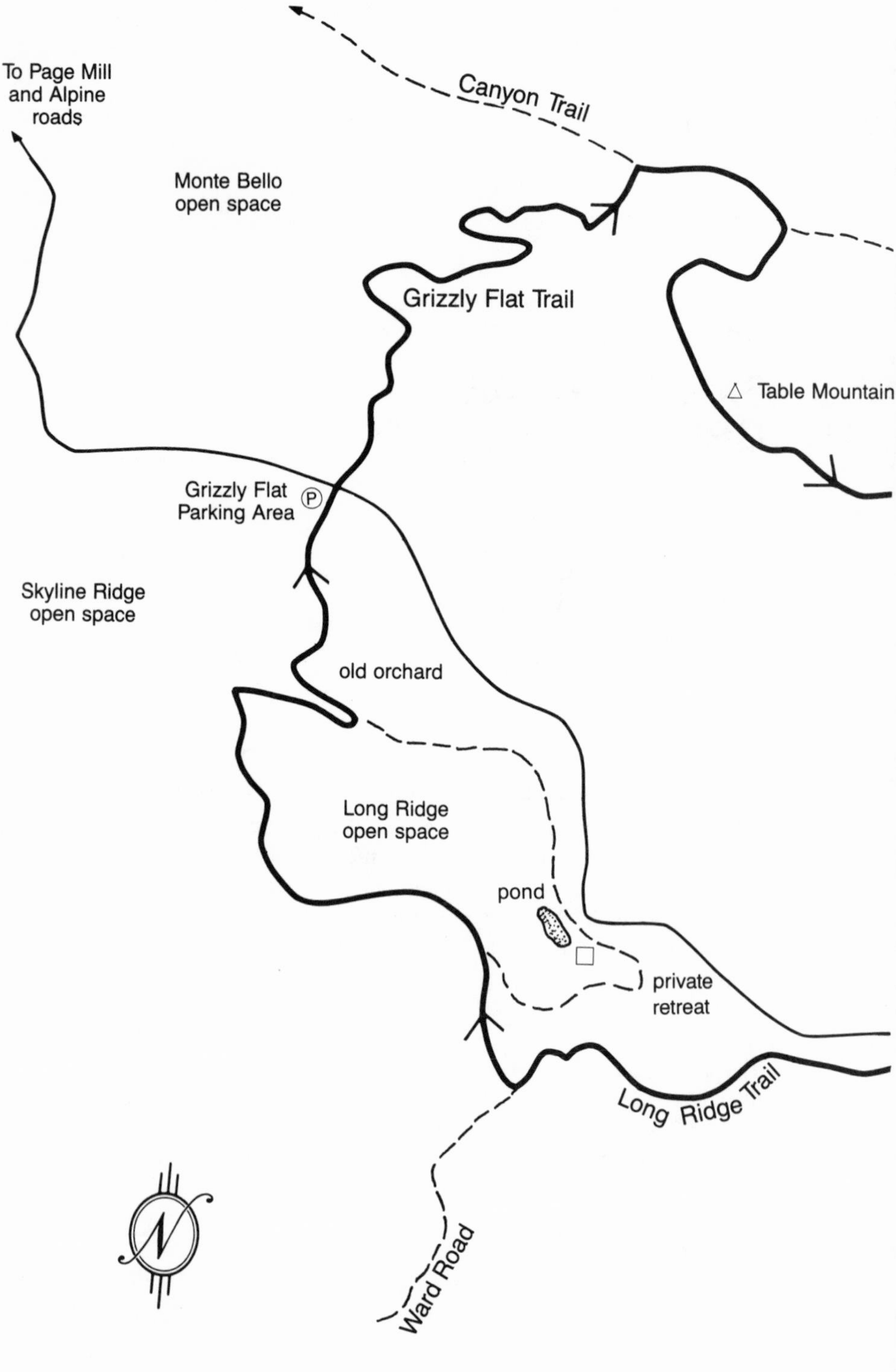

Canyon Trail

To Page Mill
and Alpine
roads

Monte Bello
open space

Grizzly Flat Trail

△ Table Mountain

Grizzly Flat
Parking Area ℗

Skyline Ridge
open space

old orchard

Long Ridge
open space

pond

private
retreat

Long Ridge Trail

Ward Road

N

# SARATOGA GAP/ GRIZZLY FLAT LOOP

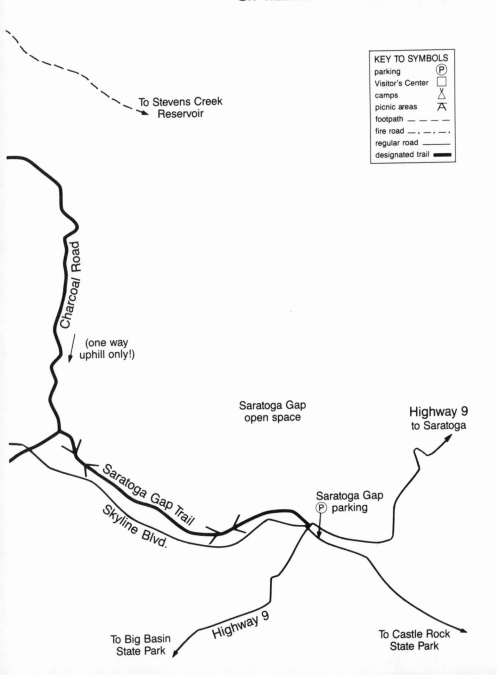

KEY TO SYMBOLS
parking ⓟ
Visitor's Center ☐
camps ⚊
picnic areas ⚊
footpath _ _ _ _
fire road _ . _ . _ .
regular road _____
designated trail ▬▬

To Stevens Creek
Reservoir

Charcoal Road

(one way
uphill only!)

Saratoga Gap
open space

Highway 9
to Saratoga

Saratoga Gap Trail

Skyline Blvd.

Saratoga Gap
ⓟ parking

To Big Basin
State Park

Highway 9

To Castle Rock
State Park

trail descends, paralleling Skyline Boulevard, through mixed forest and woodland, very fragrant early in the morning or after a rain. After nearly one mile, turn left at the intersection with Charcoal Road (you cannot go right, since Charcoal Road is open to uphill traffic only by bikes). Cross Skyline Boulevard and enter Long Ridge Open Space through the gate. Pedal approximately 1.1 rolling miles to the intersection with Ward Road.

Continue .5 miles on Long Ridge Trail to a single-track trail descending the ridge. This trail is closed to bicycle traffic during the rainy season because of muddy conditions that invite erosion problems. RESPECT THE CLOSURE! The trail drops rapidly .9 miles to a meadow where it heads left, over a stream crossing and then back up a short and moderately steep climb to Skyline Boulevard, 1.3 miles from the meadow. Cross Skyline, keeping a wary eye out for speeding vehicles, and begin a very steep descent on Grizzly Flat. Enjoy views of the grassy slopes of Monte Bello ridge that peek through the trees on occasion.

As you near the bottom of the canyon, take a look at the few remaining stands of virgin firs and maple in the area — an ideal spot for a snack break and a brief respite before embarking on the mind-bending climb up Charcoal Road. After crossing Stevens Creek, pedal up a short series of switchbacks to a right turn on the Canyon Trail. Stay on Canyon Trail for approximately .4 miles until a right turn on a trail leading to Table Mountain and Charcoal Road.

Cross Stevens Creek again and then gear down for a challenging uphill. Bike hiking is a popular alternative on this segment, which zigzags up through a forest carpeted with ferns and wild flowers in the spring. Enjoy a relatively short and moderately flat pedal around Table Mountain and then out to Charcoal Road. Bear right on Charcoal Road and gear down once again for a steep climb of just over a mile to the intersection with Saratoga Gap Trail. Turn left and head back to Saratoga Gap and the parking area.

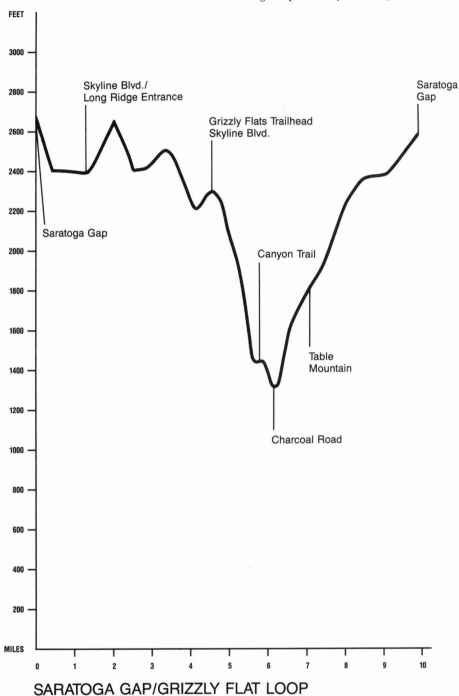

SARATOGA GAP/GRIZZLY FLAT LOOP

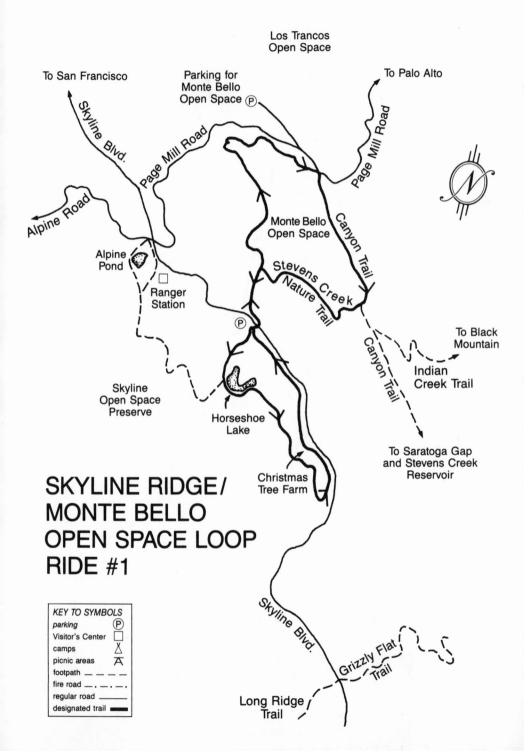

Los Trancos
Open Space

To San Francisco

Parking for
Monte Bello
Open Space Ⓟ

To Palo Alto

Skyline Blvd.

Page Mill Road

Page Mill Road

Alpine Road

Monte Bello
Open Space

Canyon Trail

Alpine
Pond

Stevens Creek
Nature Trail

Ranger
Station

Ⓟ

Canyon Trail

To Black
Mountain

Indian
Creek Trail

Skyline
Open Space
Preserve

Horseshoe
Lake

To Saratoga Gap
and Stevens Creek
Reservoir

Christmas
Tree Farm

# SKYLINE RIDGE/ MONTE BELLO OPEN SPACE LOOP RIDE #1

Skyline Blvd.

Grizzly Flat Trail

Long Ridge
Trail

**KEY TO SYMBOLS**
parking                Ⓟ
Visitor's Center   ☐
camps                  ⅄
picnic areas         ⅄
footpath              _ _ _ _
fire road              _ . _ . _
regular road        _____
designated trail   ▬▬▬

## Chapter Eight
# MONTE BELLO OPEN SPACE LOOP SKYLINE RIDGE / STEVENS CREEK COUNTY PARK

**Ride #1**
**TRAILHEAD:** *Skyline Ridge Open Space Preserve Parking Area*
**TOPO:** *Mindego Hill 7.5'*
**OVERALL DIFFICULTY:** *Moderate*
**TECHNICAL DIFFICULTY:** *Moderate*
**DISTANCE:** *Approximately 6 miles*

**Ride #2**
**TRAILHEAD:** *Stevens Creek County Park*
**TOPO:** *Mindego Hill 7.5' and Cupertino 7.5'*
**OVERALL DIFFICULTY:** *Strenuous*
**TECHNICAL DIFFICULTY:** *Easy*
**DISTANCE:** *Approximately 17 miles*

**Highlights**
Monte Bello Open Space encompasses over 2,600 acres of some of the most diverse and beautiful lands in the South Bay. Tucked in among the ridges overlooking Palo Alto, Los Altos, Los Altos Hills and Cupertino, the centerpiece of the preserve is the 2,700-foot Black Mountain and the serpentine Monte Bello Ridge. Nearly every route that winds through the preserve offers a scenic sampling of the Stevens Creek watershed from the grassy slopes of the surrounding ridges to the oak and scrub-covered woodlands. There is even a fragrant fir forest, adjacent to a Christmas tree farm on Skyline Blvd.

59

**STEVENS CREEK
COUNTY PARK/
MONTE BELLO
OPEN SPACE LOOP
RIDE #2**

*Cupertino*

To
Highway
280

Ⓟ

Stevens Creek
Reservoir

Mt. Eden Road

Monte Bello ☐
School

Monte Bello Road

Canyon Trail

Saratoga
Open Spa

To Saratoga Ga

Gold Mine Creek

Charcoal Road

Black
Mountain

Grizzly Flat Trail

Indian Creek
Trail

spring &
backpack
camp

Indian Creek

Long Ridge
Open Space

To Page Mill
Road

Monte Bello
Open Space

Skyline Blvd.

Canyon Trail

To Page Mill
& Alpine roads

To Page Mill
Road

**KEY TO SYMBOLS**
parking            Ⓟ
Visitor's Center   ☐
camps              ☖
picnic areas       ⛺
footpath           _ _ _
fire road          _ . _ . _
regular road       _____
designated trail   ▬▬▬

Skyline Ridge Open Space protects 1,250 acres of land that offer ridge top vistas, peaceful meadows and a quiet lake frequented by migrating birds.

### Getting There
From Interstate 280 and Page Mill Road in Palo Alto take Page Mill Road approximately 8 miles south to Skyline Boulevard. Turn left on Skyline Boulevard and drive about 1 mile to the Skyline Ridge Open Space Preserve parking area. Head to the right in the parking complex and park in the farthest lot, near the rest rooms and the trailhead for Horseshoe Lake and the Ridge Trail.

### The Ride
From the parking area, pedal past the sign designating the trailhead for Horseshoe Lake. At the lake, cross the wooden bridge to the left and head up a steep, but manageable .5-mile climb to the obvious entrance to the Christmas tree farm. Several dirt roads crisscross through the farm, but if you stay to the right, you will continue on the correct route. The dirt road skirts the edge of the Tree Farm, ending up paralleling Skyline Boulevard for approximately .5 miles back to the parking area and the point at which the ride crosses Skyline Boulevard and enters Monte Bello Open Space. Be extremely careful when crossing Skyline, as vehicles come up very quickly and often don't seem to be alert for bikes or pedestrians.

Once through the entrance to Monte Bello, the trail descends quickly to an intersection with Stevens Creek Nature Trail. Turn sharply to the left and continue down a steep, narrow, and winding single-track trail to Stevens Creek. During high water, the crossing can be a bit of a challenge, as rocks and boulders are concealed under water. Even at low water, staying in the saddle is creative; the drop into and climb out of Stevens Creek is lined with cobblestone to protect against erosion. Once through the creek, the trail begins to climb immediately and very steeply at times, cresting on an open hill adjacent to Page Mill Road. Look back over your shoulder for a spectacular view of the valley and mountains behind.

The trail continues to skirt the hill, ending up paralleling Page Mill Road to the parking area for Monte Bello Open Space Preserve. Pedal through the parking area and to the connecting trail for the Canyon Trail, located near the entrance from Page Mill. Do not use the trailhead at the back side of the parking area—this is only for hikers and is illegal for bikes. Pedal a short distance beside Page Mill on the dirt frontage trail to the intersection with the Canyon Trail. The descent from here is fast and furious as the road is well graded. Curb your desire for speed, however, as many others, including equestrians and hikers, use the trail.

Keep your eyes peeled for the hard right turn onto Stevens Creek Nature

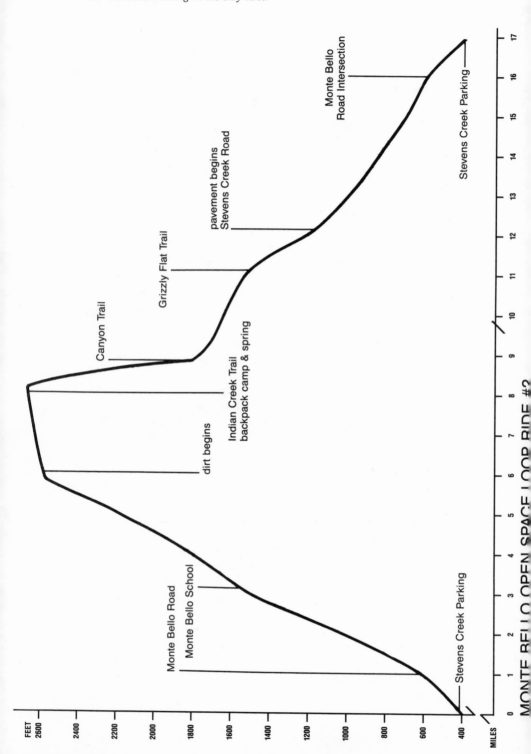

MONTE BELLO OPEN SPACE LOOP RIDE #2

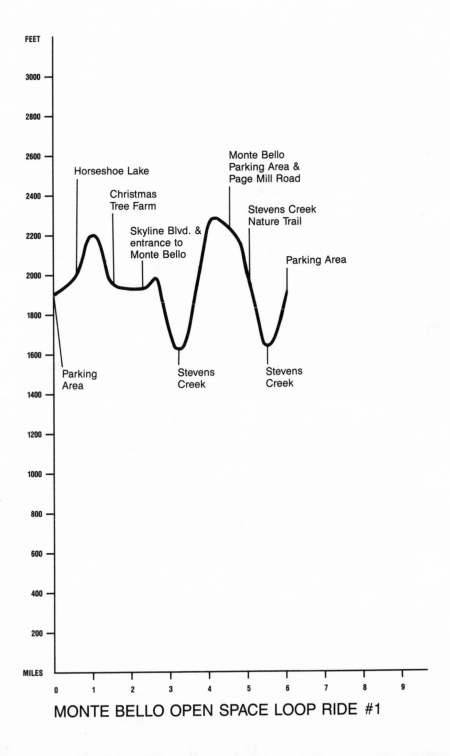

FEET

3000

2800

2600

Monte Bello
Parking Area &
Page Mill Road

Horseshoe Lake

2400

Christmas
Tree Farm

Stevens Creek
Nature Trail

2200

Skyline Blvd. &
entrance to
Monte Bello

2000

Parking Area

1800

Parking
Area

1600

Stevens
Creek

Stevens
Creek

1400

1200

1000

800

600

400

200

MILES

0   1   2   3   4   5   6   7   8   9

## MONTE BELLO OPEN SPACE LOOP RIDE #1

Trail after approximately 1 mile. Once on Stevens Creek Nature Trail, the path narrows to single track, and it becomes necessary to slow to a gentle roll as encounters with hikers are frequent. After crossing the creek over a wooden bridge, pedal uphill all the way back to Skyline Boulevard and the parking area.

### Ride #2
This ride takes the cyclist through a smorgasbord of terrain from narrow and lightly traveled paved road winding past historic buildings and wineries to dirt roads crossing golden ridges overlooking the surrounding Bay Area and streams gurgling under dense canopies of oak, madrone and fir. Spring brings with it dense carpets of flowers that bloom in brilliant succession, at times seemingly exploding out of the grassy meadows.

### Getting There
Take the Foothill Boulevard exit off of Highway 280 and head south. In approximately 3 miles Foothill turns into Stevens Canyon Road. Turn left into the park headquarters/visitor center parking area.

### The Ride
Beginning at the parking area in Stevens Creek County Park, head left on Stevens Canyon Road. Skirt Stevens Creek Reservoir on the road until turning right on Monte Bello Road. Gear down and prepare for a long haul up at times, very steep gradients. One saving grace, since the route is paved through many of the steepest sections, traction is not really an issue. Pass by both Picchetti and Ridge wineries and cycle another mile to a locked gate. Just past the gate, the pavement ends for a final grind up to Black Mountain Summit. The views from the ridge are spectacular, looking down into the valley on both sides of the road—it feels like you're on top of the world.

Just .5 mile past the peak and the airway beacon, bear left and thankfully downhill on the Indian Creek Trail. A spring and a Midpeninsula Open Space backpack camp, available by reservation sits just near the intersection of Monte Bello Road and Indian Creek. Indian Creek Trail drops steeply approximately one mile to the intersection with Canyon Trail. Bear left on Canyon Trail. Continue downhill under a canopy of leaves crossing numerous little creeks and the intersections with Grizzly Flat and Charcoal roads, finally meeting up with Stevens Canyon Road and pavement once again. Zip down the final approximately 4.5 miles, keeping a wary eye out for vehicles, back to Stevens Creek County Park and the parking area.

## Chapter Nine
# STEVENS CREEK COUNTY PARK FREMONT OLDER OPEN SPACE

**TRAILHEAD:** *Visitor Center Parking Area*
**TOPO:** *Cupertino*
**OVERALL DIFFICULTY:** *Easy/Moderate*
**TECHNICAL DIFFICULTY:** *Moderate*
**DISTANCE:** *4.5 miles*

### Highlights
Beginning in Stevens Creek County Park, the oldest county park in the system, and passing through Fremont Older Open Space, this ride offers the biker/hiker a unique escape from the nearby surrounding urban sprawl. Although the old wineries and late-18th-century settlements have long since disappeared, this area still maintains a unique blend of natural and anthropological history. Use caution on the trails, which are heavily traveled by hikers, bikers, and equestrians (there are several major stables nearby).

### Getting There
Take the Foothill Boulevard exit off of Highway 280 and head south. In approximately 3 miles Foothill turns into Stevens Canyon Road. Turn left into the park headquarters/visitor center parking area. Leave your car and head toward the trailhead for Old Canyon Trail, which begins by the visitor center.

### The Ride
Beginning at the visitor center parking area, pedal .2 mile to the trailhead for the Old Canyon Trail (actually a fire road that branches off to the left). Follow the fire road .3 mile on fairly level ground to the intersection with

65

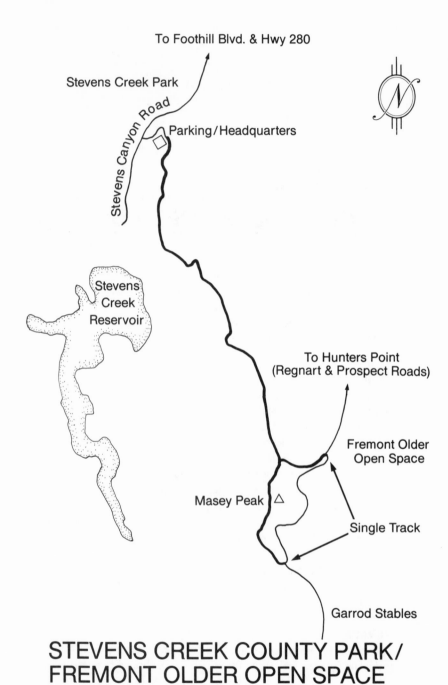

To Foothill Blvd. & Hwy 280

Stevens Creek Park

Stevens Canyon Road

Parking/Headquarters

Stevens Creek Reservoir

To Hunters Point
(Regnart & Prospect Roads)

Fremont Older Open Space

Masey Peak

Single Track

Garrod Stables

# STEVENS CREEK COUNTY PARK/ FREMONT OLDER OPEN SPACE

Rim Trail. Bear left and begin climbing. After about .6 mile and 400 feet of elevation gain, you will pedal past a trail branching off toward your left. Keep heading straight and up. Soon you will pass by private property on your left and a large water tank. Approximately .6 mile after the last trail intersection, turn left onto the cutoff trail for Regnart and Prospect roads. You will descend 160 feet in a little under .4 mile to encounter another trail branching off to your right.

While our guided ride follows this single track to the right, you do have the option of adding approximately 1.3 miles to your trip by heading left and out to Hunters Point and back. Hunters Point overlooks the bay and affords the visitor a pretty view of the city below and Moffett Field. Either way you will end up on the single track pedaling toward Garrod Stables. Follow the single track through one intersection, with trails branching right and left, straight and slightly up until you once again meet up with the fire road .8 mile later. Turn right and pedal approximately .3 mile to Masey Peak, elevation 1,160 feet. From Masey Peak it is another .4 mile downhill to the cutoff, now on your right, for Prospect and Regnart roads. From here, retrace your path to the parking area and your car. Round-trip mileage is approximately 4.5 miles.

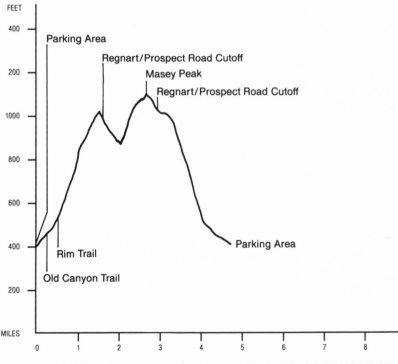

STEVENS CREEK / FREMONT OLDER OPEN SPACE

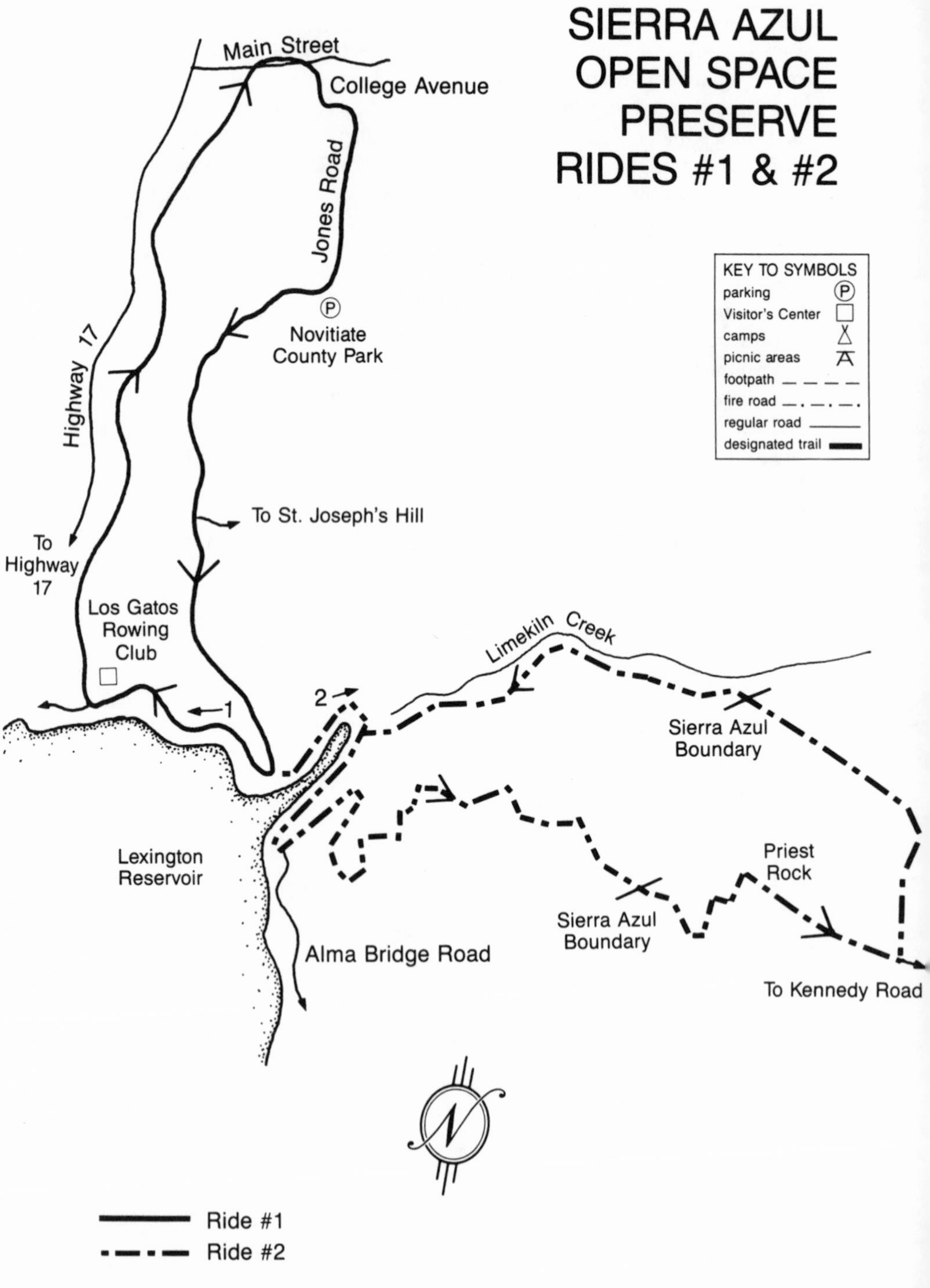
SIERRA AZUL
OPEN SPACE
PRESERVE
RIDES #1 & #2
KEY TO SYMBOLS
parking
Visitor's Center
camps
picnic areas
footpath
fire road
regular road
designated trail
Main Street
College Avenue
Jones Road
Novitiate
County Park
Highway 17
To St. Joseph's Hill
To
Highway
17
Los Gatos
Rowing
Club
1
2
Limekiln Creek
Sierra Azul
Boundary
Lexington
Reservoir
Priest
Rock
Sierra Azul
Boundary
Alma Bridge Road
To Kennedy Road
N
Ride #1
Ride #2

# Chapter Ten
# SIERRA AZUL
# OPEN SPACE PRESERVE

**TRAILHEAD:** *Novitiate County Park*
**TOPO:** *Los Gatos*

*Ride #1*
**OVERALL DIFFICULTY:** *Easy/Moderate*
**TECHNICAL DIFFICULTY:** *Easy*
**DISTANCE:** *5.3 miles*

*Ride #2*
**OVERALL DIFFICULTY:** *Strenuous*
**TECHNICAL DIFFICULTY:** *Moderate/Difficult*
**DISTANCE:** *11.1 miles*

*Ride #3*
**OVERALL DIFFICULTY:** *Very Strenuous*
**TECHNICAL DIFFICULTY:** *Difficult*
**DISTANCE:** *16 miles*

### Highlights
This open space preserve offers some of the best (and legal) riding of the Los Gatos area. The climbs are steep, the descents long and enjoyable, and the views of the Santa Clara Valley (when the smog isn't present) superb. This ride is best done in the winter (provided it hasn't recently rained), spring or fall, due to skyrocketing temperatures in the summertime.

### Getting There
From Highway 17 take the Los Gatos exit to Main Street to the east side

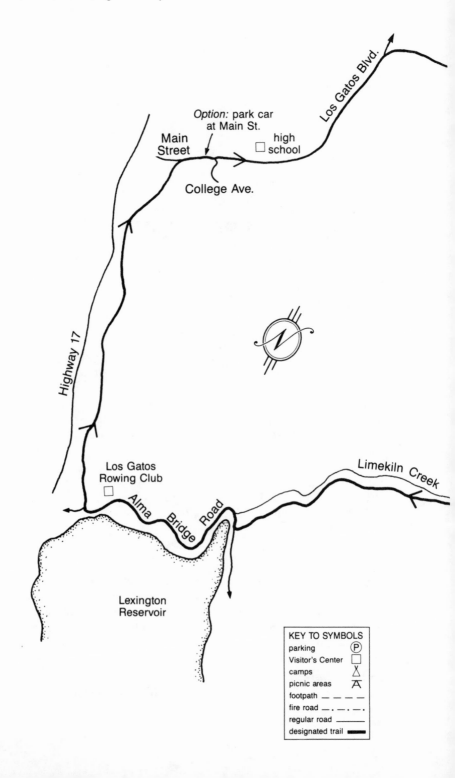

Top of the Hill Road

Kennedy Road

Ⓟ

SIERRA AZUL
OPEN SPACE PRESERVE
RIDE #3

To E. Los Gatos

Sierra
Azul

To Priest
Rock

of Highway 17. Turn right on College Avenue, go a very short distance, and then turn right on Jones Road to Novitiate Park.

### Ride #1

Beginning at the county park, ride on the popular, multi-use Jones Trail; use caution, be courteous, and give the right-of-way to walkers and runners — a warm hello is often appreciated. After a short distance an "All Must Walk" sign means just that; dismount and *walk* the short section until the next sign is encountered and then continue pedaling to the intersection with the St. Joseph's Hill Trail and turn right. Those looking for a very enjoyable though somewhat strenuous addition to this tour can take the loop to the left and add an approximate additional distance of 2.5 miles.

Continue pedaling and then prepare for an enjoyable downhill, remembering to keep your speed well under control and to let other users know you are approaching. A steep although short incline leads to a green gate and Alma Bridge Road—turn right and beware of traffic (Ride #2 turns left here). Follow the paved road for a very short distance just past the Los Gatos Rowing Club, dismount, and turn right. Pass through the gates and heed the "Walk Your Bike" signs down the incline to an intersection, where you turn left and follow the Los Gatos Creek Trail. This is a heavily used trail by runners and walkers and not the place to be testing your high gears!

Ride slowly and enjoy the scenery (or is it scene?) and please obey the signs. The Los Gatos Creek Trail leads back to Main Street in Los Gatos; turn right (again watching for traffic), ride a very short distance, and turn right on College Avenue. Follow the description for Getting There to return to your car.

### Ride #2

Follow the description in Ride #1 to Alma Bridge Road and turn left. Ride on the paved road and pass another green gate on the left (our return route will come down this), then continue pedaling 1.4 mile to the third green gate. Turn left, dismount, and pass through the gate. This is a good time to become accustomed to using some really low gears, because the climb continues for .7 mile and ascends 400 feet before leveling off and revealing great views of the valley to the north and Lexington down below.

After a short distance, prepare to again begin climbing, this time over 500 hundred feet in less than half a mile, and pass through the gate for Sierra Azul Open Space Preserve. Several turnouts, single track, and game trails will be encountered—stay on the main dirt road. You will reach an intersection 1.3 mile after the preserve gate; turn left (Ride #3 joins here) and descend.

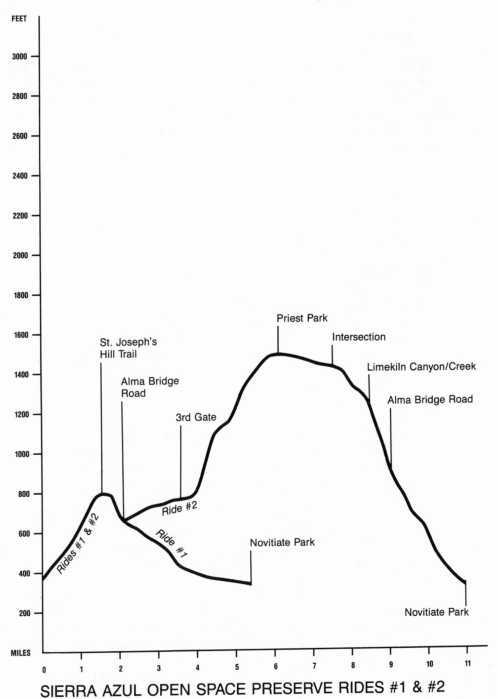

SIERRA AZUL OPEN SPACE PRESERVE RIDES #1 & #2

The next 1.5 miles are mostly downhill, steep at times, with lots of loose rocks and ruts; stay in control and keep your weight back and centered over the bike. Pass through the Sierra Azul Open Space Preserve and begin the single track. After 1.2 miles the trail climbs and drops over uneven terrain and requires some quick weight shifting—enjoy and remember that dismounting is always an option (although not always chosen!).Turn right at the intersection with Alma Bridge Road and retrace your path to your car by following the directions in Ride #1.

### Ride #3
This ride can be done as a shuttle, leaving one car at the top of Kennedy Road and the other at Novitiate County Park (see Getting There for Rides #1 and #2). Those truly wishing some additional abuse can use only one car and ride the entire loop.

### Getting There
From Highway 17 at Los Gatos, head southeast on Saratoga–Los Gatos Road to Los Gatos Boulevard and turn left. Follow a short distance to Kennedy Road and turn left. Follow Kennedy Road approximately 2.3 miles to the park entrance—look for Top of the Hill Road on the left and a very small parking area and Sierra Azul Open Space sign on the right. Parking is very limited; be certain to park well off the road when parking on the north side of Kennedy Road.

### The Ride
Pass through the gate just to the left of the private driveway and begin pedaling. After the initial very short climb, the trail then drops and follows a contour before starting its brutal climbing at approximately .5 mile. Become accustomed to the pounding in your ears and the heaving of your chest as this bear of a climb relentlessly ascends 1,800 feet in four miles. However, the trail occasionally passes through some beautiful stands of oak, maple and bay laurel trees, rewarding the visitor with some incredible views of Mount Hamilton, the Santa Clara Valley and the Diablo Range. Take some periodic rests to stop and enjoy (and it's a good excuse to catch your breath).

At mile 3.8 another road branches off to the right; continue straight and follow the roller-coaster road .6 mile to the high point—2,600 feet—congratulate yourself! In a very short distance, another intersection is encountered; stay to the right and enjoy the 1.5-mile descent to the intersection, then turn right.

Follow the description in Ride #2 to the Novitiate County Park and pass through the gate to your car; if you've opted to ride back to the top of

Kennedy Road, retrace your path back following the description in Getting There. Use extreme caution when riding on the very narrow and curved Kennedy Road. Once at the top, raise your hand and pat yourself on the back several times — you've earned it!

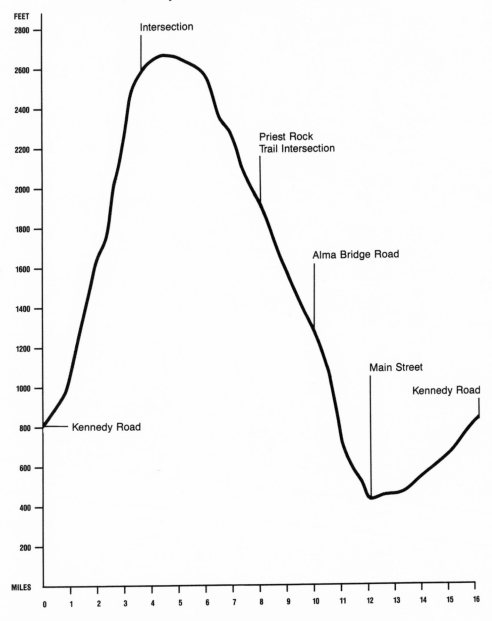

SIERRA AZUL OPEN SPACE PRESERVE RIDE #3

## Chapter Eleven
# HENRY COWELL STATE PARK

**TRAILHEAD:** *Redwood Grove Parking Lot*
**TOPO:** *Felton 7.5'*
**OVERALL DIFFICULTY:** *Moderate*
**TECHNICAL DIFFICULTY:** *Easy/Moderate*
**DISTANCE:** *9 miles*

### Description
Henry Cowell State Park is a fine ride offering a variety of terrain and climate zones, a rare vista of the Santa Cruz Mountains and the coastline, and an exciting crossing of the San Lorenzo River. Originally inhabited by Zayante Indians more than 200 years ago, this area has changed little. The beauty and solitude of the land were first protected by Henry Cowell, a prominent landowner, in 1860, and later the parcel was combined with an additional 1,500 acres and gift-deeded to the State of California by his son in 1954. While the park is best known for its giant coast redwood trees, it is also popular with swimmers and fishermen, the latter testing their skills against steelhead and silver salmon from mid-November to the end of February.

### Getting There
Just off Highway 9, 5 miles north of Santa Cruz, and 1 mile south of Felton. From Highway 17 take Mount Hermon Road 3 miles west to Graham Hill Road. Turn right and continue .5 mile to Highway 9 in the town of Felton. Turn left on Highway 9 and head south 1 mile to the day-use entrance of the Henry Cowell State Park. Turn left into the park and follow the main road to the Redwood Grove parking lot.

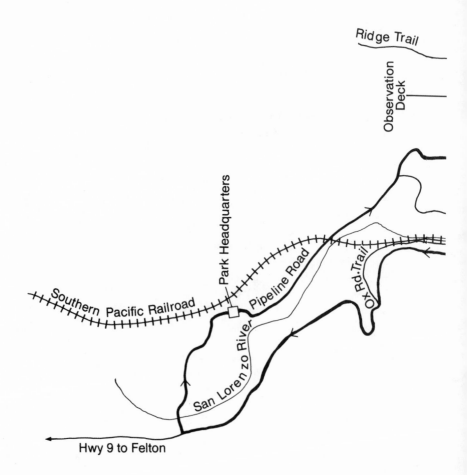

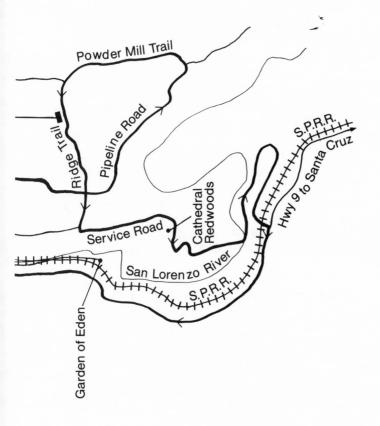

Powder Mill Trail

Pipeline Road

Ridge Trail

S.P.R.R.

Hwy 9 to Santa Cruz

Cathedral Redwoods

Service Road

San Lorenzo River

S.P.R.R.

Garden of Eden

# HENRY COWELL STATE PARK

### The Ride

Just south of the Redwood Grove parking lot is the start of your ride. Follow the service road past Redwood Grove to the trailhead for Pipeline Road. Turn left onto the paved Pipeline Road, pedaling under dense canopy for approximately .6 mile to the underpass of the Roaring Camp Railway Line. Shortly after that, and just past the Eagle Creek Trail intersection, a rather strenuous climb commences. Beginners may wish to walk until the sharp rise crests at the Ridge Trail junction. Continue straight on Pipeline Road, over rolling terrain with excellent vistas to your right of San Lorenzo Valley and brief glimpses of the ocean. After pedaling approximately 2.2 miles, bear left at Powder Mill Fire Road.

Powder Mill ascends, steeply at times, to its junction with the Ridge Fire Road. You will pass several trails branching to your right that lead to the park campground. During the climb beware of numerous sand traps. At the junction to the Ridge Fire Road bear left and up to the Observation Deck for a much-needed rest, where you will find a water fountain and an excellent lunch spot. From the deck enjoy great views of the surrounding area, including Monterey Bay and Santa Cruz to the south. If you are lucky enough to plan your ride after a rain, you will be rewarded with haze-free vistas that stretch as far as the eye can see.

Intermediate and advanced riders looking for a bit of adventure can descend the Ridge Fire Road .5 mile to Pipeline Road. Watch your speed and control; the trail is very sandy, and it is difficult to negotiate some of the steep drops and bumps. Beginners and those feeling less adventurous will turn around at the Observation Deck and retrace the route along Powder Mill Fire Road and back onto Pipeline Road to the Ridge Fire Road intersection. (To continue on the Ridge Fire Road down from Pipeline Road requires a river crossing. If, after checking with the ranger station, you discover that the San Lorenzo River is at high water, head back down the Pipeline Road to the Redwood Grove area and your car. This is also a great option for someone who is tired and wishes to shorten the ride.) From the intersection, cross the Pipeline Road and pedal .2 mile on the Ridge Fire Road over easy terrain to the intersection with Rincon Fire Road.

At the Big Rock Hole Trail/Rincon Fire Road junction, bear left on the fire road; riders are reminded to stay off Big Rock Hole Trail, which parallels the road. Gradually descending, pedal .6 mile to Cathedral Redwoods, where it is well worth dismounting and taking time to enjoy the magical splendor. After resting, the ride begins its glorious and occasionally steep descent (lower your seat post for this one) to the San Lorenzo River. Near the bottom of the valley, the fire road forks. Stay left and follow the high road. It will eventually descend to a river crossing.

Kick your shoes off and enjoy the swimming holes. When ready, hoist your bike and wade to the trail junction on the opposite side. Follow the service road up a steep climb (beginners may want to walk) approximately .5 mile to a railway crossing and Highway 9/ Trail parking area. Turn right onto Highway 9 and follow the winding road 3 miles back to the entrance of the park. Turn right onto the entrance road and go another .5 mile to the Redwood Grove parking area and your car.

On your ride up Highway 9 be cautious of traffic. You might be interested in a short .5-mile jaunt down to Ox Trail, which branches off to the right from Highway 9 at 1.5 miles. There is some decent rock scrambling and swimming to be had in the Garden of Eden at the end of the trail. You will lose about 300 feet in elevation; keep in mind you will have to pedal back up.

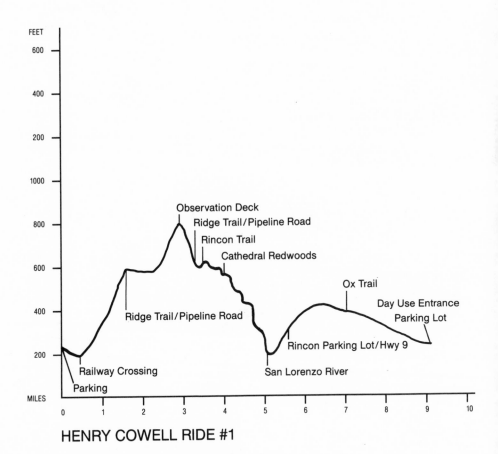

## HENRY COWELL RIDE #1

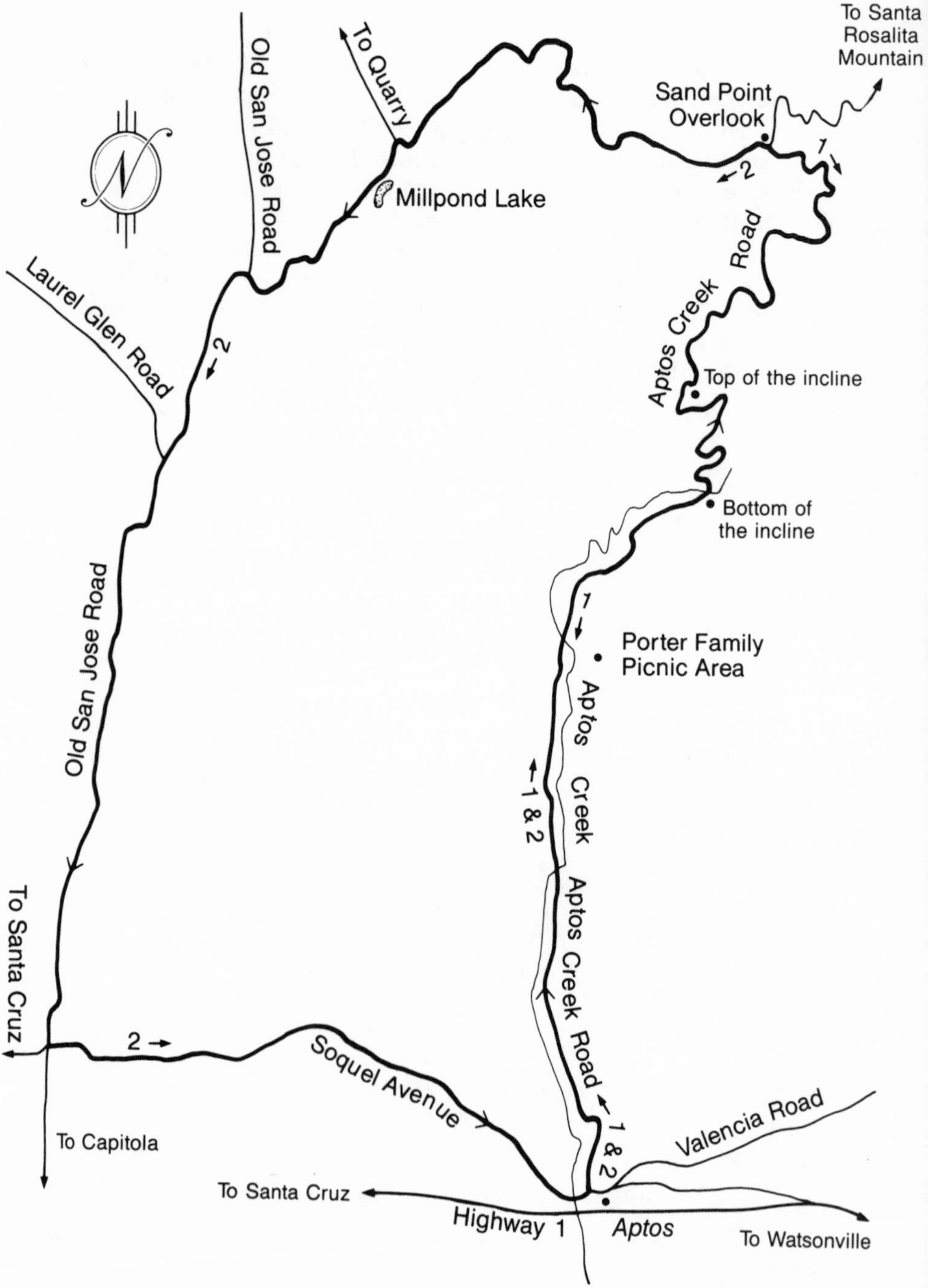

To Santa
Rosalita
Mountain

Old San Jose Road

To Quarry

Sand Point
Overlook

2

1

Millpond Lake

Aptos Creek Road

Laurel Glen Road

2

Top of the incline

Old San Jose Road

Bottom of
the incline

1

Porter Family
Picnic Area

Aptos   Creek

1 & 2

Aptos Creek Road

To Santa Cruz

2

Soquel Avenue

Valencia Road

1 & 2

To Capitola

To Santa Cruz

Highway 1   *Aptos*

To Watsonville

# FOREST OF NISENE MARKS
# STATE PARK RIDES #1 & #2

## Chapter Twelve

# FOREST OF NISENE MARKS STATE PARK

**TRAILHEAD:** *Park entrance near Soquel Drive/Aptos Creek intersection*
**TOPO:** *Soquel 7.5'; Loma Prieta 7.5'; Watsonville West 7.5'*

*Ride #1*
**OVERALL DIFFICULTY:** *Moderate/Strenuous*
**TECHNICAL DIFFICULTY:** *Moderate*
**DISTANCE:** *18 miles*

*Ride #2*
**OVERALL DIFFICULTY:** *Moderate/Strenuous*
**TECHNICAL DIFFICULTY:** *Moderate/Difficult*
**DISTANCE:** *24 miles*

*Ride #3*
**OVERALL DIFFICULTY:** *Most Strenuous*
**TECHNICAL DIFFICULTY:** *Moderate*
**DISTANCE:** *29.5 miles*

*Description*
Today's visitor to the lush surroundings of Nisene Marks State Park will have difficulty imagining the extensive clear-cutting and wanton destruction that occurred during heavy logging in the late 19th and early 20th centuries. Fortunately, 9,600 acres were purchased by the Marks family in 1950. With assistance from the Nature Conservancy, the property was donated in 1963 to the State of California. This donation was made under the condition that the natural process of restoration would continue. Much

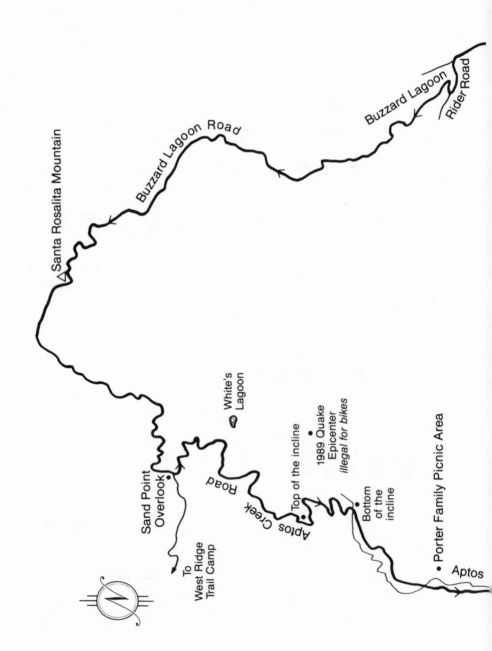

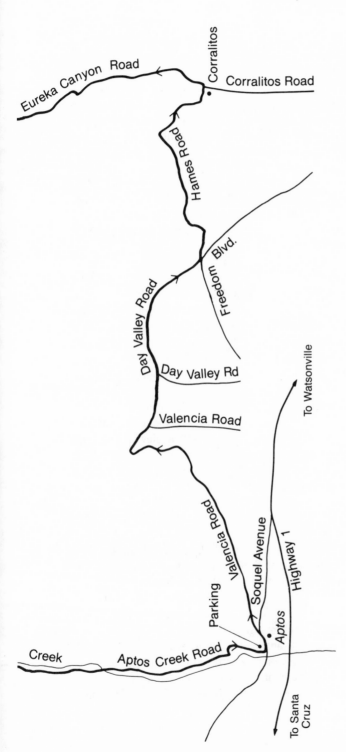

FOREST OF NISENE MARKS STATE PARK RIDE #3

of what you see today is second growth. Even the existence of what was once a small, bustling town is a distant memory and difficult to picture.

This park is a growing tribute to a forest's regenerative capability and, as stated in the State Park's brochure, "It is a forest in a state of becoming." The Forest of Nisene Marks boasts over 30 miles of hiking trails and fire roads for public use. Due to erosion and very narrow trails, mountain bikers are restricted to fire roads. Please remember, as always, you are sharing the area with other park users.

### Getting There
Take Highway 1 to the Seacliff Beach/Aptos exit. Follow State Beach Road north .25 mile to Soquel Drive and turn right. Continue .5 mile to Aptos Creek Road, turn left, and park at the turnout on the right past the railroad tracks.

### Ride #1
Begin pedaling .8 mile up a paved road that turns into dirt for another 2.2 miles to Porter Family Picnic area. This is an excellent resting point for those desiring a more leisurely trip. Continue another .7 mile on the fire road to the Loma Prieta Mill site with remains of the old mill foundation and mill pond. From the mill site it is another .8 mile to Aptos Creek, where the road will begin to climb in earnest; those wishing to keep their ride easy will want to turn around here.

At Aptos Creek the road climbs from 380 to 962 feet in about 1.5 miles, cresting atop China Ridge. Continue climbing at a more gradual pace approximately 3 miles to Sand Point Overlook and an elevation of 1,600 feet. Enjoy the view from the best vantage point in the park, with vistas of Santa Cruz, Monterey Bay, UC-Santa Cruz, and Ben Lomond Ridge. After you have rested, return the way you came. Be sure to stay to the right and control your speed.

### Ride #2
Begin Ride #2 from the Sand Point Overlook. Bear left downhill to West Ridge Trail Camp, approximately .5 mile and 150 feet of elevation loss. Continue down on the Hinkley Fire Road to the gate .9 mile from the trail camp. Watch out for multiple cross drainages that will bury your front wheel and introduce your face to a nearby tree. Keep your weight over the back wheel and keep a relaxed grip on the handlebars.

From the gate, ride .2 mile to an intersection, where you will bear right. Pedal .3 mile to another intersection, where you will once again bear to the right. Notice the signs indicating private property. Please respect the owner's privacy. From here the ride goes through a series of three stream

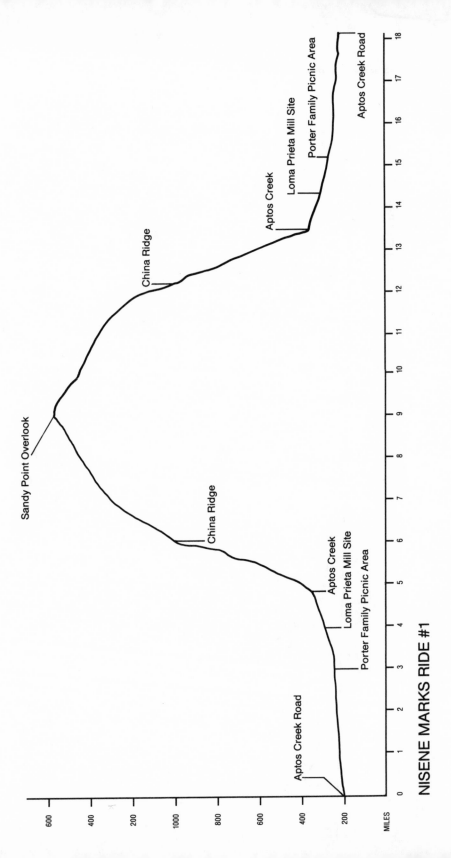

NISENE MARKS RIDE #1

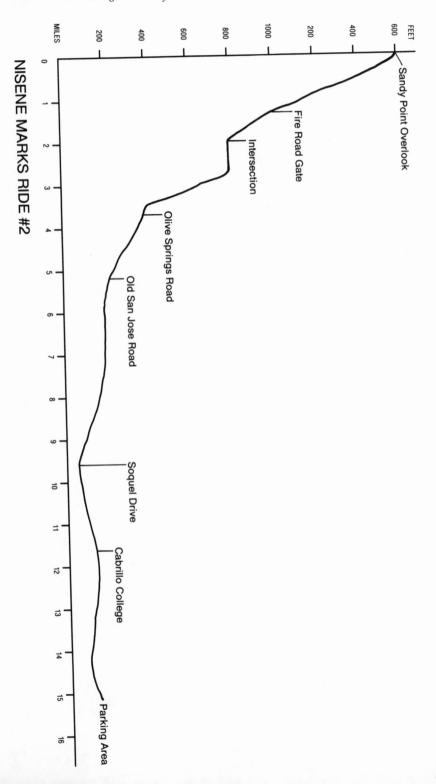

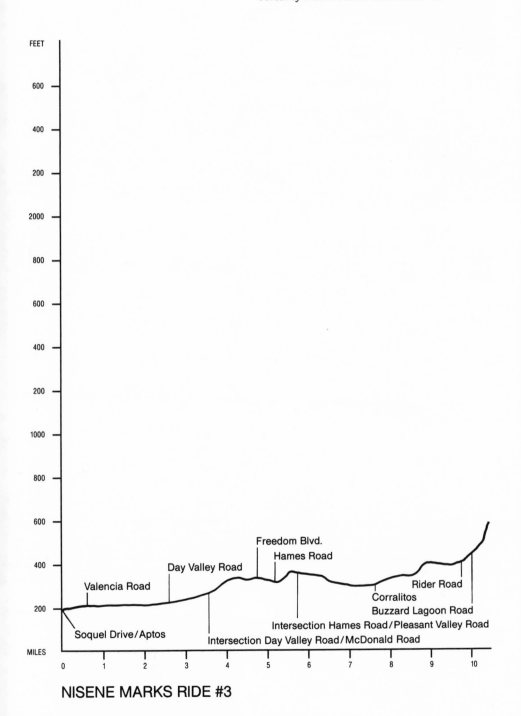

**NISENE MARKS RIDE #3**

NISENE MARKS RIDE #3

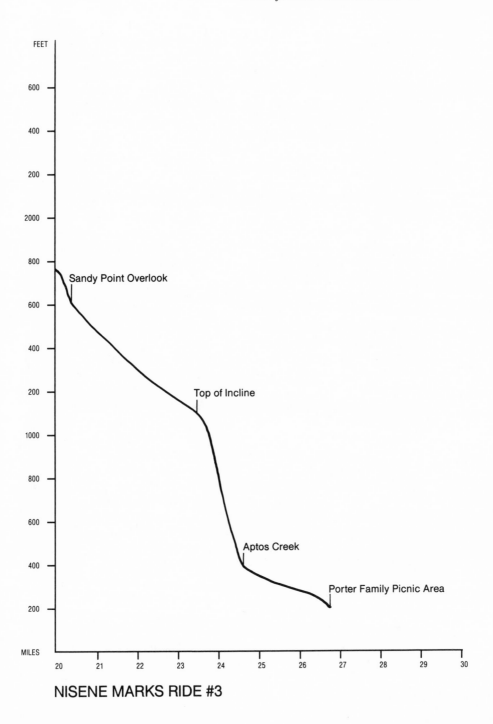

**NISENE MARKS RIDE #3**

crossings that are guaranteed to wet your feet and bring a smile to your face. Continue .4 mile downhill to Olive Springs Road, where you will turn left past a small weight station. Ride 1.2 miles along a scenic and rural road to a left turn on Soquel–San Jose Road. Riders are reminded to use extreme caution due to heavy traffic. Soquel–San Jose Road will take you down to the intersection with Soquel Drive and the town of Soquel. Turn left on Soquel Drive and an easy 3.5-mile pedal back to the parking area and your car.

### Ride #3

Begin Ride #3 at the turnout and your car. Turn left (east) on Soquel Drive. Ride .1 mile to Trout Gulch Road and turn left. Continue .5 mile to Valencia Road, turn right and pedal 2.6 miles to Day Valley Road. Turn right again and climb gradually through open fields and farmland .8 mile to the intersection of McDonald and Day Valley roads. Stay to the left and cycle 1.3 miles to Freedom Boulevard (exercise caution on this heavily used road) and Day Valley Road intersection. Turn left and pedal .2 mile on Freedom Boulevard to Hames Road and a short uphill climb.

Following the climb, the road begins to descend .7 mile to the intersection of Pleasant Valley and Hames roads. Bear left and remain on Hames Road for an easy .2-mile descent. The road levels and you will continue for another 1.5 miles to a left turn on Eureka Canyon Road and the town of Corralitos.

Take advantage of the store for a cool drink and a snack if your body requests refueling. From here the road climbs and rolls gently 2.2 miles to Rider Road and Eureka Canyon intersection. Turn left on Rider Road and pedal approximately .3 mile to Buzzard Lagoon Road. Buzzard Lagoon Road climbs steadily, changing to dirt half way up, until reaching the overview at 3.5 miles and an approximate elevation of 2,132 feet. Continue to the Buzzard Lagoon/Aptos Creek Fire Road intersection at 1.3 miles. Bear left on Aptos Creek Fire Road 1 mile to a locked gate. Lift your bike over and continue climbing .8 mile to the highest point in Nisene Marks. Enjoy the view and catch your breath.

From the overview it is all downhill to your car via the Sand Point Overlook. Losing 2,300 feet in just under 12 miles will paste a smile on your face for sure. Please use caution, however, as many others are using the trail for hiking, biking, and playing. CONTROL YOUR SPEED! Word to the wise: Ride #3 covers approximately 29 miles. Do not try this ride unless you are in very good shape and plan on starting early in the day.

## Chapter Thirteen
# HENRY COE STATE PARK

**TRAILHEAD:** *Henry Coe State Park Headquarters*
**TOPO:** *Mississippi Creek; Mount Sizer*

*Ride #1*
**OVERALL DIFFICULTY:** *Easy*
**TECHNICAL DIFFICULTY:** *Easy*
**DISTANCE:** *5.4 miles*

*Ride #2*
**OVERALL DIFFICULTY:** *Moderately strenuous*
**TECHNICAL DIFFICULTY:** *Moderately difficult*
**DISTANCE:** *9.5 miles*

*Ride #3*
**OVERALL DIFFICULTY:** *Most strenuous*
**TECHNICAL DIFFICULTY:** *Moderately difficult*
**DISTANCE:** *15.3 miles*

### Highlights
Essentially a wilderness park, this 68,000-acre preserve is a hidden gem in the San Francisco Bay region. With elevations ranging from 710 to 3,560 feet, Henry Coe Park offers mixed grassland, oak and pine forests on steep ridges, and deep canyons. Springs, streams, and numerous reservoirs provide much-needed water for the abundant wildlife. Deer, raccoons, skunks, foxes, bobcats, wild turkeys, wild pigs, and the occasional mountain lion all make their home within the park's boundaries. Fall colors and spring wild flowers make these the best seasons to visit the park.

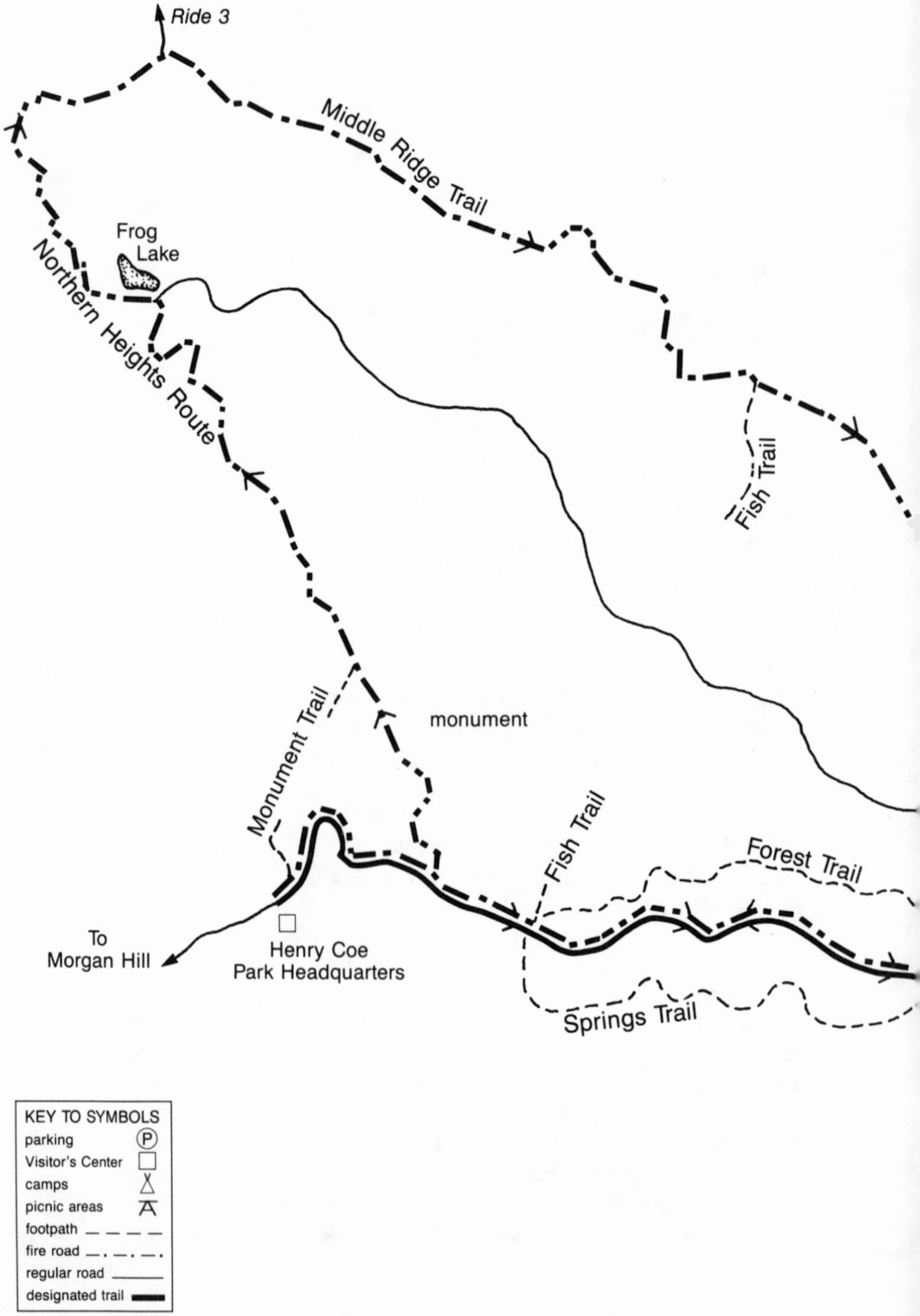

Ride 3

Middle Ridge Trail

Frog Lake

Northern Heights Route

Fish Trail

Monument Trail

monument

Fish Trail

Forest Trail

To Morgan Hill

Henry Coe Park Headquarters

Springs Trail

KEY TO SYMBOLS
parking          Ⓟ
Visitor's Center  ☐
camps           ⋏
picnic areas     ⩏
footpath        _ _ _ _
fire road       _ . _ . _ .
regular road    _____
designated trail  ▬▬▬

# HENRY COE STATE PARK
# RIDES #1 & #2

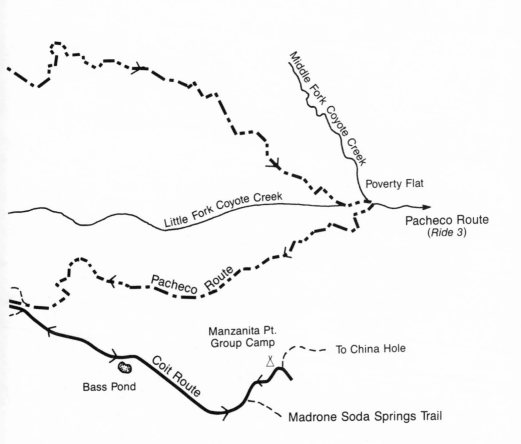

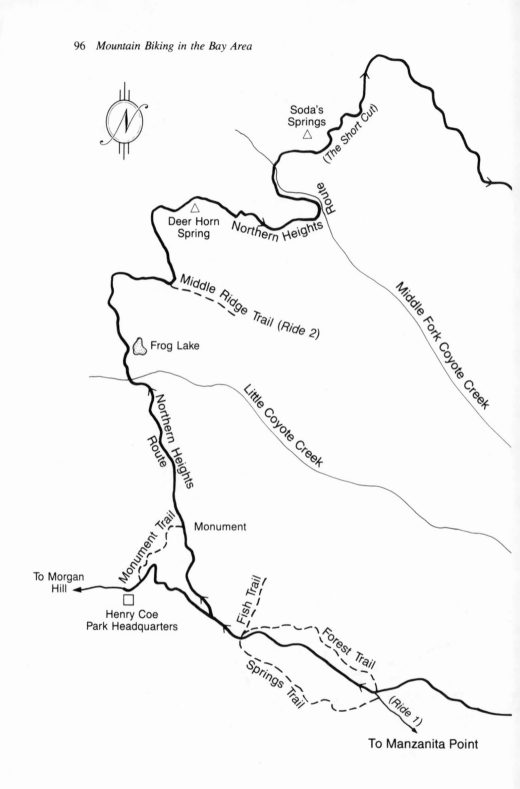

# HENRY COE STATE PARK
# RIDE #3

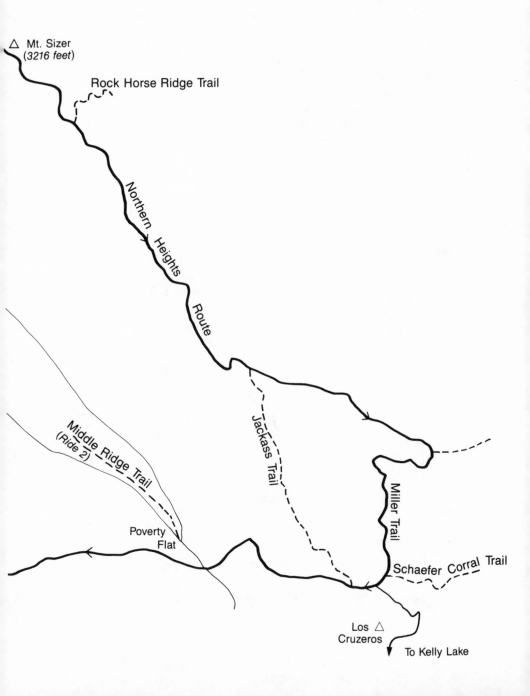

△ Mt. Sizer
*(3216 feet)*

Rock Horse Ridge Trail

Northern Heights Route

Jackass Trail

Middle Ridge Trail
*(Ride 2)*

Miller Trail

Poverty Flat

Schaefer Corral Trail

Los △ Cruzeros

To Kelly Lake

The summers are hot and dry and winters often wet with frequent frost and some snow.

Unfortunately, little is known about the original inhabitants who frequented the area thousands of years before the arrival of Spanish explorers in the 18th century. Several camps or village sites of the Costanoan Indians have been discovered within the boundaries of the park. More recently, 1776 to be exact, Juan Bautista de Anza named the major creek in the area Arroyo del Coyote; this has since been changed to Coyote Creek. American influence in the Santa Clara Valley to the west came during 1846 in the form of cattle ranching and wheat growing.

When the railroad was added to the valley, fruit growing began to replace wheat and cattle, so the ranchers moved higher into the hills. The 12,500-acre Pine Ridge Ranch of pioneer Henry Coe became a county park in

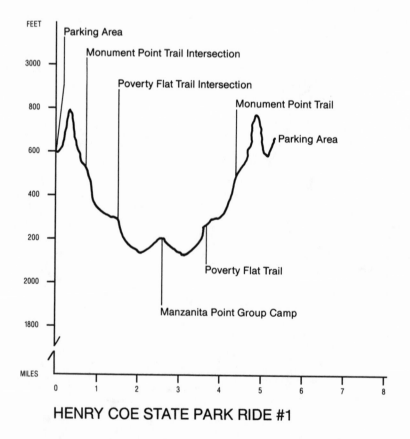

HENRY COE STATE PARK RIDE #1

1953, when it was donated by Coe's daughter. The park was turned over to the state in 1958, and since that time, several adjacent ranches have been purchased and added to the park.

Much of the park is remote wilderness. Trails and roads are steep, rocky, and sometimes treacherous. Caution is the word, and control is the key. We feel that only one ride is suitable for beginners, with the remainder ideal for strong intermediates and above. In terms of beauty and solitude, this park rates as one of our favorites.

The solitude dictates that riders be prepared for the unexpected. Two water bottles and a water-purification system are essential. Springs and streams are abundant in the park, but the water must be treated before drinking. Water may be scarce in summer and fall when most streams and some springs are dry. A basic tool kit and small first-aid kit are strongly recommended (see appendix for listing of contents). For maximum enjoyment, start early in the day and plan your turnaround to coincide with a time, not a destination. There are numerous backcountry campsites in the park available to bikers; call the park headquarters for information at 408-779-2728.

It was Sada Sutcliffe Coe's wish that the park provide "peace for one's soul and food for the power of thought." We think that you will find, no matter what your venture, the peace that she wished.

### Getting There
From Highway 101 take the East Dunne Avenue exit bearing east at Morgan Hill. Follow the signs up a narrow, winding 13-mile road past Anderson Reservoir to its dead end at the park headquarters.

### Ride #1
This is the only ride suitable for beginners. We recommend bringing a picnic lunch and enjoying the solitude and view to be had at Manzanita Point Group Camp. From the park headquarters, ride through the Pacheco Route gate and up a fairly easy incline, gaining 200 feet toward Manzanita Point and Poverty Flat. At .7 mile, the Northern Heights Route Fire Road branches off to the left (Rides #2 and #3 begin here and continue up toward the Monument and Frog Lake).

Continue straight and downhill to the intersection with Pacheco Route and Coit Route fire roads at 1.5 miles. Stay right, continuing on a rolling road to the sign for China Hole Trail (Ride #2 description starts here). Bear left and pedal several hundred yards to the turnaround at the trailhead for Rabbit Spring and the farthest point in Manzanita Point Group Camp. The mileage to this point is 2.7. Enjoy the views and your lunch and then return the way you came. Round-trip mileage is approximately 5.4 miles.

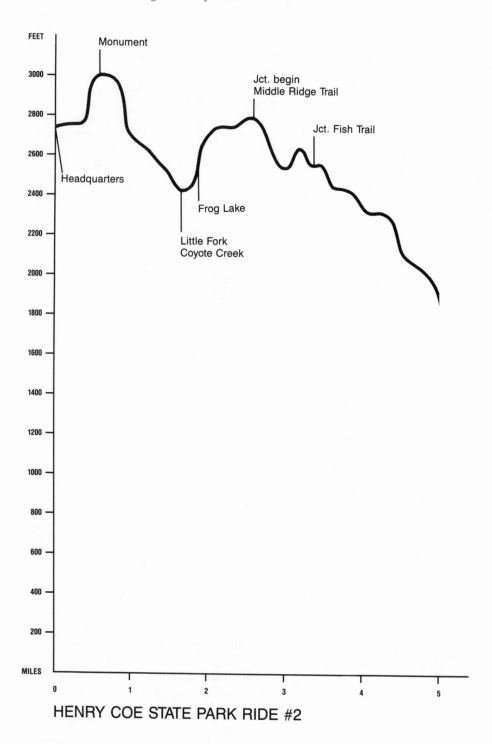

HENRY COE STATE PARK RIDE #2

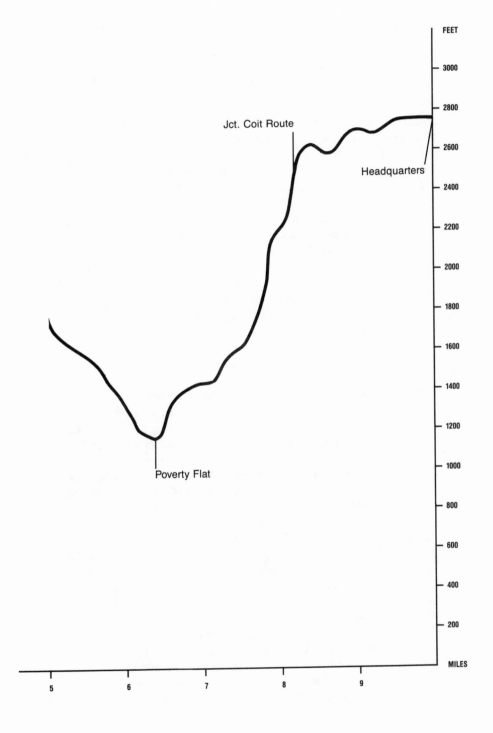

### Ride #2

The Middle Ridge Loop is a popular 9.5-mile ride that is truly intermediate in level — it is recommended to anyone who believes they are in good shape but have never ridden Coe's ridiculously steep roads and trails before.

The loop starts as with Ride #1, but turns left at the Northern Heights Route fire road. At the top of Middle Ridge, .8 mile after Frog Lake, turn right on single track Middle Ridge Trail. Enjoy the 1.7 miles of rolling ridge riding, with a few short moderately steep sections. Watch out for the stiff sharp branches of red-barked manzanitas that can be less than forgiving on human skin! After reaching an open grassy area, the trail then turns and begins to descend more rapidly down the east slope of the ridge. This wild 1.5 mile section drops more than 1,000 feet through shady open woods and includes some steep switchbacks — use care and remember all those downhill techniques your mother taught you.

At the bottom of the hill, cross the Middle Fork of Coyote Creek. This brings you to the west end of Poverty Flat, a worthwhile place for a refreshing dip (highly recommended considering the climb that's ahead) if the creek still has water in it. From here the path crosses the stream and begins a mind-bending climb, gaining 1,100 feet in just under 1.8 miles to the intersection with Coit Route. Once at the top, it's homeward bound over a fairly level 1.5 miles back to your car.

### Ride #3

Beginning at the Monument cutoff from Ride #1, climb approximately 400 feet in .5 mile to the Monument and intersection with a hiking trail branching off to the left. Continue straight toward Frog Lake. The road descends steeply about 600 feet over the next mile until leveling out below the reservoir (an old cattle pond). From here the fire road follows a rolling track (climbing and dropping 200 feet) 1.3 miles to Deer Horn Springs. Lower your seat and prepare for a wild and woolly 900-foot elevation loss in 1.1 miles, bringing you to the cutoff for Upper Camp.

Raise your seat and brace yourself for some serious mountain bike walking — straight up Short Cut Road to Blue Ridge Fire Road and the turnoff for Mount Sizer. Once at the top, look back. You have just walked your bike up about 1,500 feet in just under 1.3 miles. Bear right and continue for approximately 1 mile and the intersection with the road up Mount Sizer; it is worth the short pedal to the top of the 3,200-foot summit, one of the highest points in the park.

Pedal on for almost 2 miles over relatively level terrain with spectacular vistas to the north and south. The trail then descends rapidly, losing 1,000 feet over the next 2 miles until reaching the intersection with Los Cruzeros to the left (east) and Poverty Flat up and to the west. Consult Ride #2 for trail description through Poverty Flat and back to your car.

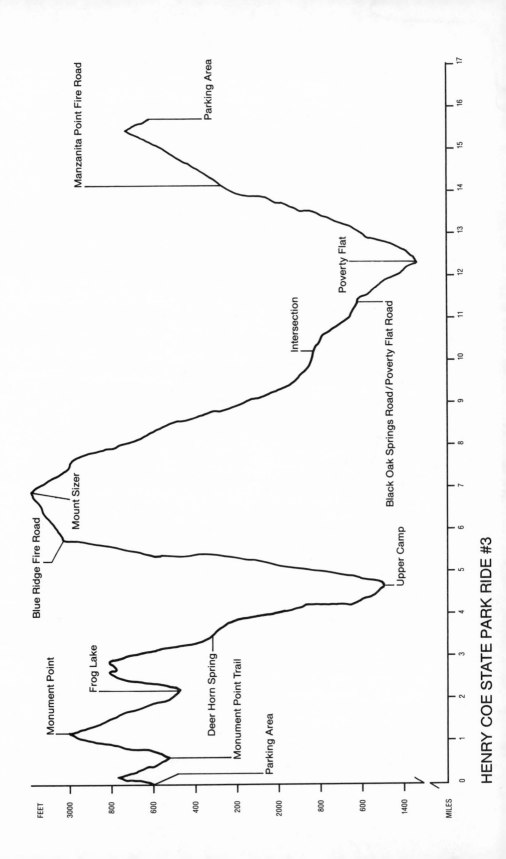

HENRY COE STATE PARK RIDE #3

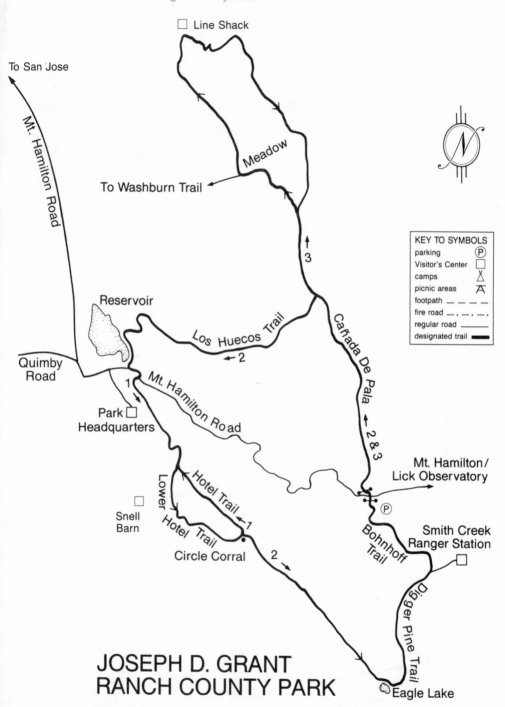

□ Line Shack

To San Jose

Mt. Hamilton Road

Meadow

To Washburn Trail

Reservoir

Los Huecos Trail

← 2

3

Cañada De Pala

← 2 & 3

KEY TO SYMBOLS
parking                    Ⓟ
Visitor's Center           □
camps                      △
picnic areas               ⩑
footpath                   _ _ _
fire road                  _._._.
regular road               _____
designated trail           ▬▬▬

Quimby
Road

Park □
Headquarters

Mt. Hamilton Road

1

Hotel Trail

Lower Hotel Trail

← 1

Snell □
Barn

Circle Corral

2 →

Mt. Hamilton /
Lick Observatory

Ⓟ

Bohnhoff Trail

Smith Creek
Ranger Station
□

Digger Pine Trail

◉ Eagle Lake

# JOSEPH D. GRANT
# RANCH COUNTY PARK

## Chapter Fourteen

# JOSEPH D. GRANT RANCH COUNTY PARK

*Ride #1*
**TRAILHEAD:** *Visitor's Center*
**TOPO:** *Lick Observatory; Mount Day*
**OVERALL DIFFICULTY:** *Easy*
**TECHNICAL DIFFICULTY:** *Easy*
**DISTANCE:** *2.5 Miles*

*Ride #2*
**TRAILHEAD:** *Visitor's Center*
**TOPO:** *Lick Observatory; Mount Day*
**OVERALL DIFFICULTY:** *Strenuous*
**TECHNICAL DIFFICULTY:** *Moderately Difficult*
**DISTANCE:** *9.6 miles*

*Ride #3*
**TRAILHEAD:** *Bohnoff and Canada de Pala Trails*
**TOPO:** *Lick Observatory; Mount Day*
**OVERALL DIFFICULTY:** *Moderate*
**TECHNICAL DIFFICULTY:** *Easy*
**DISTANCE:** *8.5 miles*

### Description

Joseph D. Grant Ranch County Park is a frequently overlooked jewel within Santa Clara County. Though livestock grazing takes place on much of the park, there is ample room for hikers, equestrians, and, of course, mountain bikers. The park is located in the Mount Hamilton range very near the Lick Observatory. The landscape is rich and colorful with rolling grasslands, magnificent oak woodlands, and spectacular vistas of the surrounding mountains. Lush and green in the spring or golden and subtle in the fall, this park is worth experiencing. Keep a careful eye open for wildlife as you pedal along, and you just might be rewarded with a view of a golden eagle hunting the fields or a bobcat melting into the shadows.

### Getting There

Just south of the 280/880 interchange on 101 take the Tully Road exit heading east. Stay on Tully until you reach Quimby Road and turn right. Quimby Road narrows just before heading into the foothills and winds approximately 4 miles until the intersection with Mount Hamilton Road. At Mount Hamilton Road bear right; you will see the park entrance in approximately .25 mile on your right. For Rides #1 and #2 enter the park and leave your car near the visitor center. For Ride #3 continue driving 3.5 miles up Mount Hamilton Road to a dirt parking area next to the road and the trailhead for the Bohnoff and Canada de Pala trails. It is important to remember that these trails are used by everyone and you as a responsible mountain biker must yield the right-of-way to pedestrians and equestrians. (*Note: the county of Santa Clara now requires all cyclists using trails to wear a helmet—a citation may be issued for noncompliance.*)

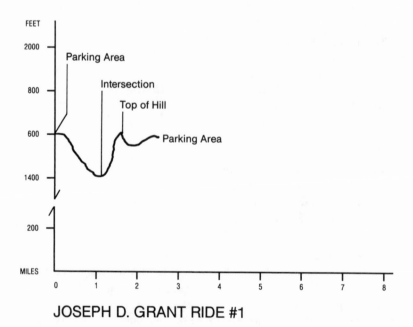

## JOSEPH D. GRANT RIDE #1

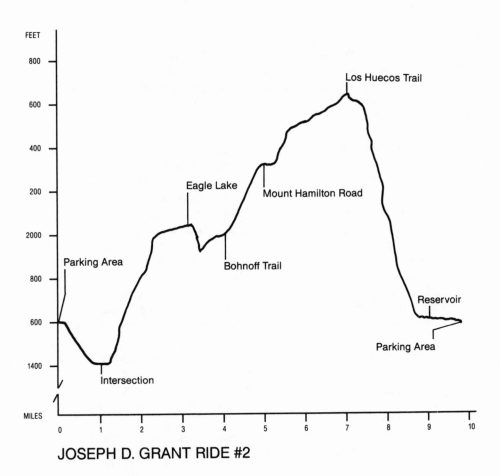

FEET

800

600 — Los Huecos Trail

400

200 — Eagle Lake — Mount Hamilton Road

2000

Parking Area — Bohnoff Trail

800 — Reservoir

600 — Parking Area

1400 — Intersection

MILES
0   1   2   3   4   5   6   7   8   9   10

# JOSEPH D. GRANT RIDE #2

### Ride #1

Beginning at the visitor center parking area, go east through two livestock gates and the start of the Hotel Trail. The Lower Hotel and Hotel trails form a 2.5-mile loop that is well suited for beginners. Approximately .2 mile from the last gate bear right on the Lower Hotel Trail along the corral fence. The trail descends gradually 1 mile until meeting up once again with the Upper Hotel Trail at the Circle Corral. (Ride #2, for intermediate-to-advanced riders, continues right, climbing the Hotel Trail to Eagle Lake.)

Bear left on Hotel Trail for an elevation gain of 160 feet in .75 mile. At the top of the hill you have an option of taking a side trip to Bass Lake, a decision we will leave up to your sense of adventure. Hotel Trail descends 160 feet in .25 mile from the hilltop and rejoins the main trail for the return to the parking area.

### Ride #2

Follow the trail description for Ride #1 until the Circle Corral. This ride has very steep ascents and challenging descents, making it suitable only for intermediate and advanced riders. You are guaranteed to feel your pulse on this one, and walking is to be expected.

From Circle Corral bear right into the trees, where the trail immediately begins to climb. From this point you will gain 680 feet in 1.75 miles to Eagle Lake. It is every bit as hard as it sounds as the dirt is loose and rutted. There are several flat sections in between the climbs — not enough to catch your breath but just long enough to give you hope.

At Eagle Lake take time to have lunch; it is a beautiful spot with excellent vistas among the oaks. If you are fatigued or looking to make this a short trip, head back the way you came, controlling speed, to the parking area. Continuing on, head left at Eagle Lake, where the trail makes a quick, but short 160-foot descent into a cool canyon. Following the stream bed for a brief period, the Digger Pine Trail (named for the stand of Digger pines you pass near the crest of the ridge) becomes quite rocky with a number of short but intense ascents. One mile from Eagle Lake turn left on the Bohnhoff Trail for yet another steep ascent. (We didn't even bat an eye and walked this one.)

After about a 400-foot elevation gain, the trail levels out quickly and meanders along the ridge before making a quick descent to Mount Hamilton Road, .8 mile from Digger Pine. There is a gate on either side of the road — please be sure to secure them. You are now on the Canada de Pala Trail, heading north. The trail immediately tests your legs as it climbs 200 feet in approximately .2 mile. Once you reach the top of the ridge, your efforts are rewarded with 360-degree views of the surrounding foothills.

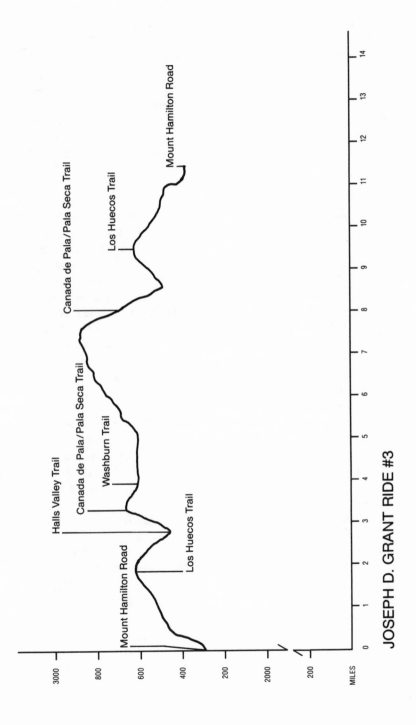

JOSEPH D. GRANT RIDE #3

The trail continues another rolling 1.5 miles along the ridge until the intersection with Los Huecos Trail. (Ride #3 will continue straight along the Canada de Pala Trail at this point.) Turn left for a wild and woolly 1.7-mile descent, losing 840 feet to the reservoir. Use caution: halfway down, after a short uphill and in a somewhat flat area, you will encounter a barbed wire fence that requires lifting your bike or opening the gate. After reaching the lake, turn left to Mount Hamilton Road. At the road bear left and in approximately .1 mile turn right, through a gate, and head .3 mile back to the parking area. Congratulations! You have just completed a 9.6-mile loop.

### Ride #3

Approximately 3.5 miles from the main park gate on Mount Hamilton Road you come to a dirt parking area on the right side of the road. From here cross over the road (to the north side) and through the gate to begin the ride. This tour is suitable for advanced beginners all the way to experienced riders. Follow the directions for Ride #2 beginning at Mount Hamilton Road to the Los Huecos Trail. At the Los Huecos Trail continue straight on Canada de Pala, losing 180 feet in .8 mile to the Halls Valley Trail. From here you will gain 200 feet in .4 mile to the intersection of Canada de Pala and Pala Seca Trail. Bear left, continuing on Canada de Pala, which remains fairly flat with a slight descent into a wonderful meadow.

After .6 mile the trail meets with the Washburn Trail (illegal for bikes) and continues right, along the border of the meadow. The next 1 mile parallels a stream for a wonderfully cool and refreshing canyon ride. All too soon, however, the trail leaves the shade and climbs approximately 100 feet to a line shack used when herding cattle. At the shack bear right along a faint trail. You are now on the Pala Seca Trail, which climbs steeply 200 feet to the top of the ridge, giving one the feeling of being on top of the world.

From the line shack back to the Canada de Pala Trail is 2.1 miles. The descent from the ridge to the intersection is rapid and steep, but not too difficult. Once back on the Canada de Pala Trail, turn left and retrace your path to Mount Hamilton Road gate and parking area.

## Chapter Fifteen

# SAN FRANCISCO BAY
# NATIONAL WILDLIFE REFUGE

*Ride #1*
**TRAILHEAD:** *Visitor's Center Parking Area*
**TOPO:** *Mountain View 7.5'; Newark 7.5'*
**OVERALL DIFFICULTY:** *Easy*
**TECHNICAL DIFFICULTY:** *Easy*
**DISTANCE:** *5 miles with a 7-mile loop option*

*Ride #2*
**TRAILHEAD:** *Alviso Slough Parking Area*
**TOPO:** *Mountain View 7.5'; Newark 7.5'*
**OVERALL DIFFICULTY:** *Easy*
**TECHNICAL DIFFICULTY:** *Easy*
**DISTANCE:** *8.7 miles*

*Description*
Established in 1972, this 23,000-acre wildlife refuge is easily overlooked while speeding by on the local freeways. Those who are willing to take the time to pedal along the levees and shorelines will discover a city-bounded wilderness teeming with life. Birds are perhaps the most obvious denizens, with more than 250 species using this habitat during the course of a year, most abundantly during the fall and winter. Given time and patience, one may also view a hidden world of striped bass, crabs, harbor seals, and even the occasional otter. It might be of interest to you, as it was to us, that acre for acre, salt water marshes outproduce our best farms for nutrients. These marshes are not wastelands as they are often viewed. It is worth your time to take a peek, but remember to keep your eyes and ears peeled.

# SAN FRANCISCO BAY NATIONAL WILDLIFE REFUGE
## RIDE #1

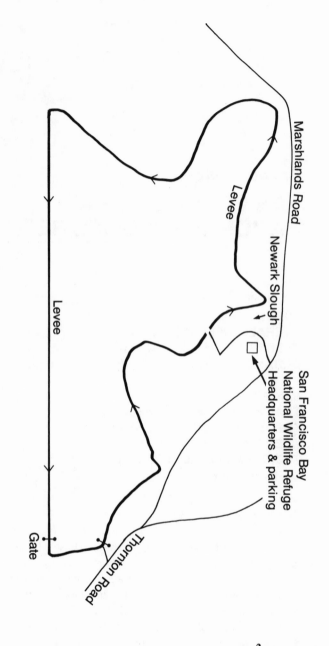

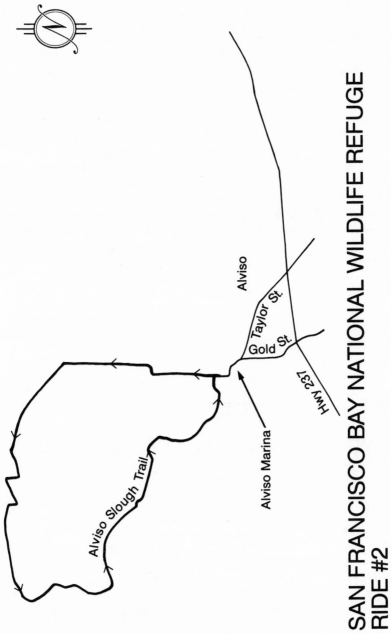

SAN FRANCISCO BAY NATIONAL WILDLIFE REFUGE
RIDE #2

### Getting There
*Visitor Headquarters in Fremont:* From 880 or 101 take Highway 84 to the east end of the Dumbarton Bridge. Take the Thornton Avenue exit, follow it south for .5 mile, and turn right onto Marshlands Road into the visitor center parking area. Now follow the directions for Ride #1 outlined below.

*Alviso Entrance:* From Highway 237, east of 880 and north of 101, take the North First Street exit and head north. Bear right on Gold Street and drive two blocks until making a left turn on Elizabeth Street. Drive two blocks on Elizabeth, then make a right turn on Hope Street, which will take you into the trailhead parking area. It can get somewhat confusing in here, but your ultimate goal is the Alviso Marina parking area. Stay alert and you will get there. Now follow the directions for Ride #2.

### Ride #1
Though this ride definitely has a beginner level of difficulty, the area's abundant wildlife and serenity provide enjoyment for all riders. There are two trails to ride in this part of the refuge. Starting and finishing at the visitor center, the Tidelands Walking Trail completes a 1.4-mile loop with a short

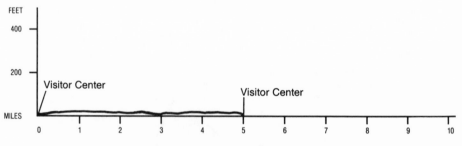

SAN FRANCISCO BAY WILDLIFE REFUGE RIDE #1

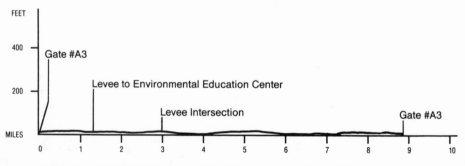

SAN FRANCISCO BAY WILDLIFE REFUGE RIDE #2

but steep hill. There are walkers and birders present, so watch your speed.

The second trail, called the Newark Slough Trail, begins just below the visitor center across a wooden access bridge. This trail is a very flat and easy 5-mile loop through the Newark Slough and affords the visitor numerous opportunities to view the birds, sea life, and mammals that frequent the area.

### Ride #2

Beginning at gate #A3, head out onto the Alviso Slough Trail for an 8.7-mile loop that will end back at this gate. Don't be turned off by the industrial appearance; the terrain will improve within 1.4 miles to that of a true saltwater marsh. At 1.4 miles, a levee veers off to the right across the railroad tracks and will take you to the Environmental Education Center, which is currently closed on weekends but may be open in the future. This levee as well as others are closed off periodically to protect wildlife. Please observe all signs, as violators will be fined. For the purpose of our ride continue north. At 3 miles a levee branches off to the left; this levee rejoins the main trail 1.2 miles north of the parking area and is an option to shorten your ride if you wish. From here just follow the trail through open slough, mud flats, and saltwater marsh back to the parking area and a finishing mileage of 8.7. Birders, casual or otherwise, won't want to leave their binoculars or birding books behind on this ride.

## Chapter Sixteen
# COYOTE HILLS REGIONAL PARK

**TRAILHEAD:** *Coyote Hills Parking Area*
**TOPO:** *Newark 7.5'*
**OVERALL DIFFICULTY:** *Easy*
**TECHNICAL DIFFICULTY:** *Easy*
**DISTANCE:** *8.6 miles with an option to add 2.6 or 1.4 miles*

### Description
Coyote Hills is a 1,039-acre wildlife sanctuary located at the south end of San Francisco Bay near Fremont. This area has an extensive history dating back almost 2,300 years. The diet of the Native Americans living on this land consisted mostly of shellfish, as evidenced by the four shell mounds visible today. In addition to its rich history, the park's resources include grassy hills, freshwater marshes, and seasonal wetlands. During periods of migration and in the winter, this area becomes a bird-watcher's paradise. Don't forget, this park is a wildlife sanctuary, so please keep to the trails and leave everything as you found it. Although the rides in this refuge are mostly flat and easy, we feel the scenic beauty will appeal to all levels of bikers. We recommend an early-morning visit to take advantage of smaller crowds, cooler temperatures, and more visible wildlife.

### Getting There
Just west of Highway 84 and Interstate 880 lies Coyote Hills. Take the Paseo Padre Parkway, exit at Highway 84, and head north. Follow it to Patterson Ranch Road and turn left to the park entrance and the dirt parking area directly following.

### The Ride
From the parking area and the information kiosk, ride .5 mile on the bike

117

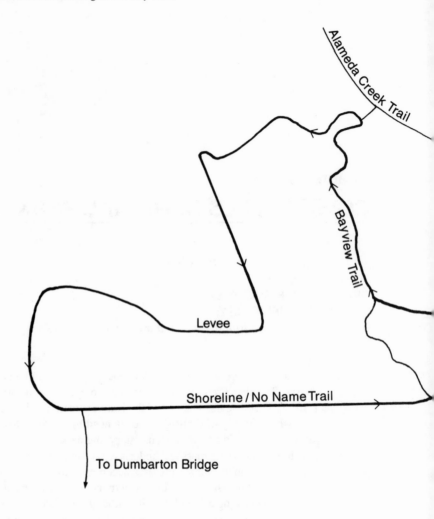

Alameda Creek Trail

Bayview Trail

Levee

Shoreline / No Name Trail

To Dumbarton Bridge

# COYOTE HILLS REGIONAL PARK

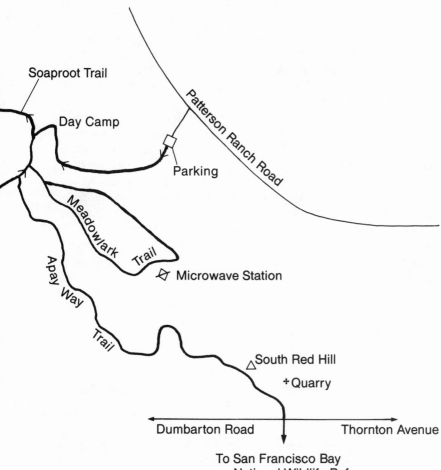

Soaproot Trail

Day Camp

Patterson Ranch Road

Parking

Meadowlark Trail

Apay Way Trail

⊠ Microwave Station

△ South Red Hill

+ Quarry

Dumbarton Road          Thornton Avenue

To San Francisco Bay
National Wildlife Refuge

path paralleling Patterson Ranch Road. Turn left at the Alameda Creek Ponding Area and head toward the Day Camp and Quarry on the Bayview Trail. At the Day Camp, the trail makes a sharp hairpin. Head west (left) immediately after the hairpin on the Soaproot Trail, which becomes a dirt road and climbs steeply until its crest and intersection with the Red Hill Trail (illegal for mountain bikes).

You will quickly lose elevation until your abrupt rejoining of the Bayview Trail (watch your speed). Turn right on the Bayview Trail and continue until meeting up with the Alameda Creek Trail. You have gone 2.3 miles to here and may turn back to the parking area by bearing right on the Bayview Trail.

For those continuing on, head left and onto the sand levee of the Alameda Creek Trail/Shoreline Trail. At 5.8 miles the path turns into No Name Trail. Dumbarton Bridge Trail branches right (to the south) and intersects with Marshlands Road, if you are feeling adventurous. Otherwise, continue on the No Name Trail until you once again rejoin the Bayview Trail at 7.2 miles. Follow the Bayview Trail to Patterson Ranch Road and your car with an ending mileage of approximately 8.6.

If you wish to add distance and, of course, scenic beauty, we recommend riding up and back on Apay Way Trail (2.6 miles) and/or Meadowlark Trail Loop (1.4 miles). Apay Way Trail is fairly flat dirt road with a gradual incline during the first .4 mile. The turnaround point is the toll booth at the bridge crossing Highway 84. Should you wish to extend your ride even farther, it is possible to ride over the bridge and tour the San Francisco Bay National Wildlife Refuge (see Chapter Fifteen for more detailed information). Meadowlark Trail is not for the faint of heart; the first .6 mile climbs very steeply to a microwave station. You will have just enough time to catch your breath before a rapid descent to the marsh and a rejoining with Bayview Trail at 1.4 miles.

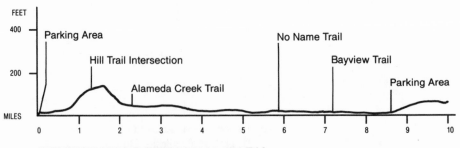

COYOTE HILLS REGIONAL PARK

## Chapter Seventeen
# ANTHONY CHABOT
# REGIONAL PARK

**TRAILHEAD:** *Chabot City Park/West Shore Trail*
**TOPO:** *Oakland East, Las Trampas Ridge, Hayward*
**OVERALL DIFFICULTY:** *Moderate*
**TECHNICAL DIFFICULTY:** *Easy*
**DISTANCE:** *Approximately 13.6 miles*

### Highlights
Probably best known for its fishing and boating, Anthony Chabot is an excellent park for hiking, biking, and equestrian use. It is also well known for Chabot Family Camp, with tent, trailer, and walk-in campsites. The camp has hot showers and is a first-class base for exploring the park and surrounding environment. Call 510-635-0135 for more information.

Chabot Regional Park is a 4,927-acre preserve named after Anthony Chabot, the California businessman who created Lake Chabot by building an earthen dam. Originally frequented by Indians for food gathering, the lands were later used for cattle ranching. In the early 1900s the region was converted into watershed lands for the city of Oakland by the People's Water Company. The water company later became the East Bay Municipal Utility District in 1928 and now leases the lake to the park for public use.

While the area around the lake itself is quite crowded, especially on weekends, the inland trails away from the lake offer miles of excellent biking through grasslands, chaparral, and shady eucalyptus groves. The East Bay Skyline National Trail, crossing more than 31 miles of East Bay land from Richmond to Castro Valley, runs the length of Anthony Chabot and is open to mountain bikes while in the park.

### Getting There

Located just east of Interstate 580 and Oakland International Airport. Take the Fairmont Drive exit and follow Fairmont Drive to a left turn on Lake Chabot Road (to the right is the parking for Lake Chabot Marina). Turn right on Estudillo Avenue and head over the narrow bridge into the parking area for the City of San Leandro Chabot Park. The trailhead is beyond the gate at the far end of the parking area.

### The Ride

Beginning at the parking area, ride through the gate and up .6 mile on a paved fire road to the intersection with Bass Cove Trail and West Shore Trail. Bear right on West Shore Trail for 1.8 miles of rolling and paved road to the Lake Chabot Marina. Exercise extreme caution through here as there are lots of hikers, bikers, and fishermen using the trail. At the Marina bear left on the East Shore Trail and ride 1.4 rolling miles to the intersection with Cameron Loop and the end of the paved trail. Pedal another .2 mile to the second junction with Cameron Loop heading right and proceed across a narrow bridge to the left. Once over the bridge, bear right up the Live Oak Trail 1.2 miles to the junction with the Towhee Trail on the right and a road heading left to the Anthony Chabot Family Campground.

Continue right and up the Towhee Trail to the top of the ridge and the intersection of Brandon and Redtail trails. Turn left onto the Redtail Trail and continue past a day-use parking area, the Marksmanship Range, and another intersection with the Brandon Trail bearing left; continue past the Marciel Staging Area and descend to the intersection with the Grass Valley Trail—total mileage on the Redtail, 2.1 miles. At the Grass Valley Trail we recommend taking time for a picnic lunch on one of the grassy spots near the stream. When ready, pedal 1 mile along the relatively flat Grass Valley Trail through several cattle gates and to the Bort Meadow Staging Area. Head left and now back up the other side of the valley on the Brandon Trail.

(If you wish a very long ride it is possible to continue straight 2.3 miles on the East Bay Skyline Trail instead of turning left on the Brandon Trail. This will connect you with Redwood Regional Park and Redwood Road. Bear right on Redwood Road and pedal to the park office and the Canyon Meadow Staging Area, where you can join our described Redwood Park ride at the Canyon Trail. The Redwood Loop is approximately 8.3 miles, so this would make for quite a long but enjoyable day — be prepared and start early.)

Continue pedaling 1.8 miles past the cutoff to the equestrian center and the stone bridge and up the Jackson Grade to the intersection with

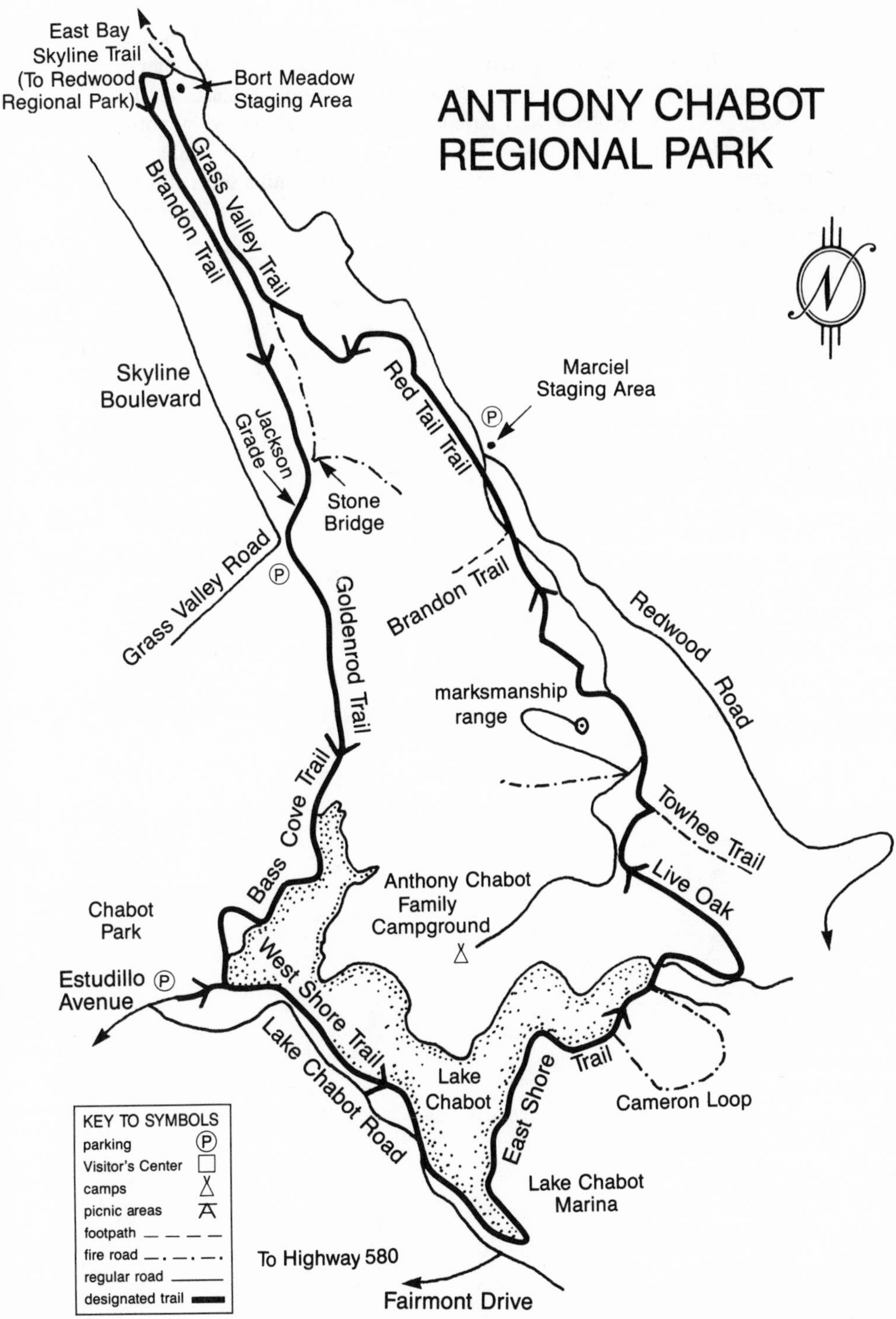
ANTHONY CHABOT
REGIONAL PARK
East Bay
Skyline Trail
(To Redwood
Regional Park)
Bort Meadow
Staging Area
Grass Valley Trail
Brandon Trail
Skyline
Boulevard
Jackson
Grade
Red Tail Trail
Marciel
Staging Area
Stone
Bridge
Grass Valley Road
Goldenrod Trail
Brandon Trail
Redwood
Road
marksmanship
range
Bass Cove Trail
Towhee Trail
Live Oak
Anthony Chabot
Family
Campground
Chabot
Park
Estudillo
Avenue
West Shore Trail
Lake Chabot Road
Lake
Chabot
East Shore
Trail
Cameron Loop
Lake Chabot
Marina
To Highway 580
Fairmont Drive
KEY TO SYMBOLS
parking
Visitor's Center
camps
picnic areas
footpath
fire road
regular road
designated trail

Goldenrod Trail and a day-use parking area on Skyline Boulevard. Head left on Goldenrod Trail for a gradual, though steady, descent to the intersection with Bass Cove Trail 1.4 miles later. (Use caution, because at 1.1 miles you will encounter a brief paved section that is also used by golf carts from the nearby golf course.) Bear left on the Bass Cove Trail and descend 1.1 miles to the lake. Proceed along its banks until a short climb and the intersection with West Shore Trail. Turn left on the paved fire road and head down to the parking area.

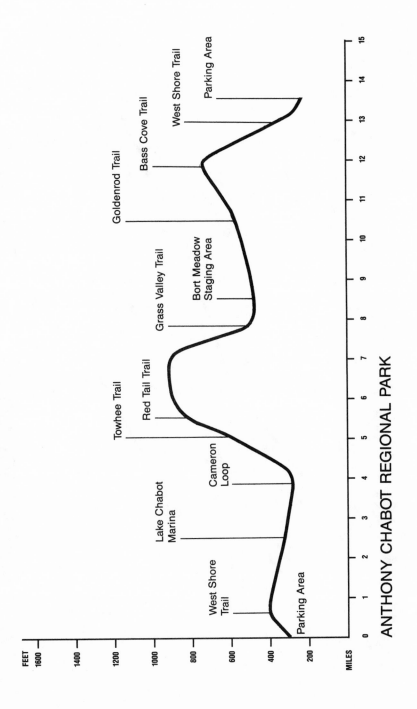

ANTHONY CHABOT REGIONAL PARK

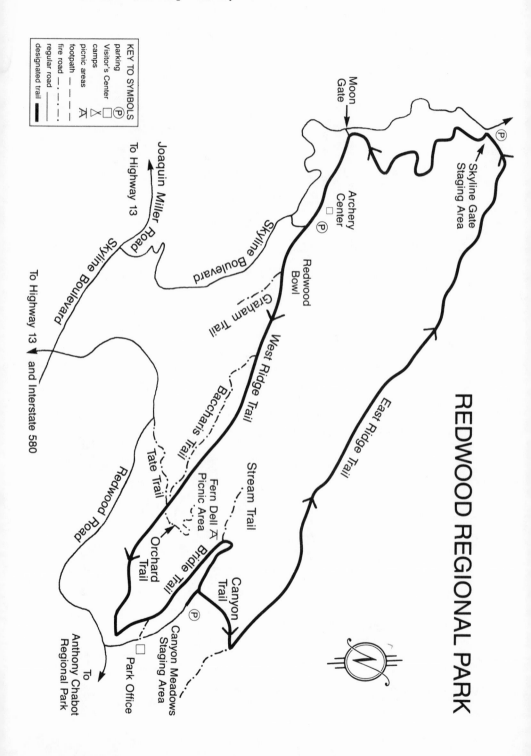

KEY TO SYMBOLS
parking                              Ⓟ
Visitor's Center                     ▢
camps                                △
picnic areas                         🅰
footpath               — — — —
fire road              —..—..—..
regular road           —————
designated trail       ▬▬▬▬

REDWOOD REGIONAL PARK

Moon Gate

Skyline Gate Staging Area

To Highway 13

Joaquin Miller Road

Skyline Boulevard

Skyline Boulevard

To Highway 13 and Interstate 580

Archery Center

Redwood Bowl

Graham Trail

West Ridge Trail

East Ridge Trail

Baccharis Trail

Tate Trail

Redwood Road

Fern Dell Picnic Area

Stream Trail

Orchard Trail

Bridle Trail

Canyon Trail

Canyon Meadows Staging Area

Park Office

To Anthony Chabot Regional Park

N

## Chapter Eighteen
# REDWOOD REGIONAL PRESERVE

**TRAILHEAD:** *Canyon Trail, Canyon Meadow Staging Area*
**TOPO:** *Oakland East*
**OVERALL DIFFICULTY:** *Moderate/Strenuous*
**TECHNICAL DIFFICULTY:** *Moderate*
**DISTANCE:** *8.5 miles*

### Highlights

Redwood Regional Park is a peaceful escape from the nearby noise and
congestion of downtown Oakland. The park also boasts the unique distinc-
tion of being the spot where rainbow trout were first identified as a distinct
species. The protected trout still spawn in Redwood Creek after migrating
from a downstream reservoir outside of the park; fishing is prohibited.
Redwood Regional Park is perhaps best known for its magnificent stands
of 150-foot-plus coast redwoods, the *Sequoia sempervirens.* In 1826 the
ship logs of the Royal Navy indicated that several of the huge redwoods
were used as navigational landmarks from sightings made 16 miles away
at what is now Golden Gate. While much of the park was heavily logged
in the mid-1800s, the second-growth stand of redwoods remains impressive.
The 1,830-acre park also includes evergreen, chaparral, and open grasslands. If you start your ride early enough in the morning, before the throngs
begin hitting the trail, you stand a good chance of seeing deer, raccoon,
and perhaps the rare golden eagle hunting rabbit or squirrel. There are
several group camping areas available within the park; call 510-635-0135
for more information.

### Getting There

Just east of Oakland and Highway 13. Take Highway 13 to Redwood Road
(just north of the intersection of Highway 13 and Interstate 580). Turn east

on Redwood Road, crossing over Skyline Boulevard to a left turn at the Redwood Gate Park Entrance. Leave your car at the Canyon Meadow Staging Area. The trailhead begins by Owl Picnic Area just to the north end of the staging area.

### The Ride

Beginning at the trailhead for Canyon Trail, pedal up a fairly short but steep .5 mile to the intersection with East Ridge Trail. This section is somewhat muddy in the winter and may require step-by-step slogging. At the East Ridge Trail, bear left for a gentle 3.3-mile climb to the Skyline Gate Staging Area. From the staging area you will continue straight, now on the West Ridge Trail, 1.2 miles of gentle climbing with spectacular views off to the east. At Moon Gate the trail climbs sharply and then levels for a rolling .8-mile ride to the Redwood Bowl. Just past the Bowl, and at the intersection with West Ridge and Graham Trail, bear left and continue on West Ridge for 1 mile of very fun and gentle downhill and rapid whooptydoo rocky stair steps — pick your route carefully and you should be able to stay in the saddle.

At the intersections with Tate and Baccharis trails, both branching right, West Ridge begins a 1.6-mile quick and sometimes quite steep descent down to the Bridle Trail. The track is loose and muddy in places, so stay in control and watch your speed. Once on the Bridal Trail, head left to a stone bridge and the Fern Dell Picnic Area, and then turn right on the road back to the Canyon Meadow Staging Area and your car, .8 mile later.

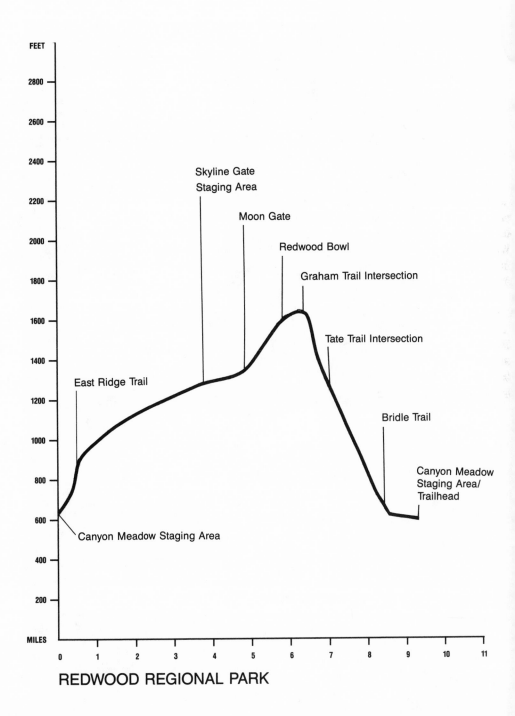

FEET

2800

2600

2400

Skyline Gate
Staging Area

2200

Moon Gate

2000

Redwood Bowl

1800

Graham Trail Intersection

1600

Tate Trail Intersection

1400

East Ridge Trail

1200

Bridle Trail

1000

800

Canyon Meadow
Staging Area/
Trailhead

600

Canyon Meadow Staging Area

400

200

MILES

0   1   2   3   4   5   6   7   8   9   10   11

## REDWOOD REGIONAL PARK

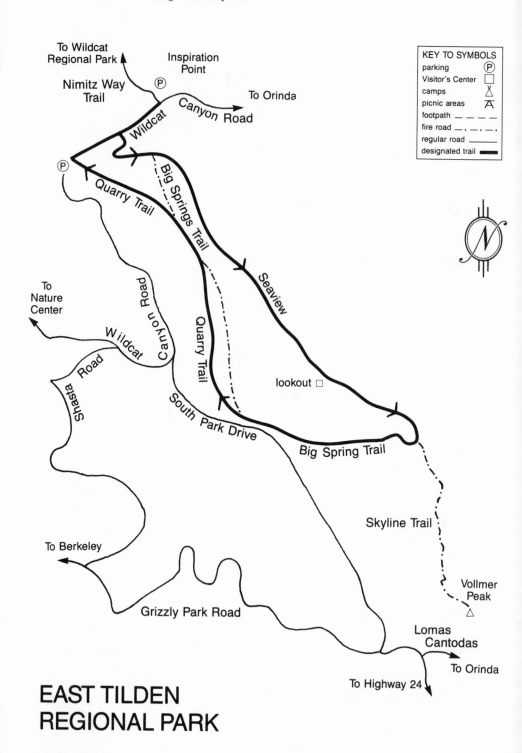

KEY TO SYMBOLS
parking        Ⓟ
Visitor's Center   ☐
camps       ⋏
picnic areas   ⚊
footpath _ _ _ _
fire road _ . _ . _ .
regular road _____
designated trail ▬▬▬

To Wildcat
Regional Park
Inspiration
Point
Nimitz Way
Trail
Ⓟ
To Orinda
Canyon Road
Wildcat
Ⓟ
Big Springs Trail
Quarry Trail
Seaview
Canyon Road
To
Nature
Center
Wildcat
Quarry Trail
Shasta Road
lookout ☐
South Park Drive
Big Spring Trail
Skyline Trail
To Berkeley
Grizzly Park Road
Vollmer
Peak
△
Lomas
Cantodas
To Orinda
To Highway 24

# EAST TILDEN
# REGIONAL PARK

## Chapter Nineteen
# EAST TILDEN REGIONAL PARK

**TRAILHEAD:** *Seaview Trail*
**TOPO:** *Briones Valley*
**OVERALL DIFFICULTY:** *Easy/Moderate*
**TECHNICAL DIFFICULTY:** *Easy*
**DISTANCE:** *Approximately 3.7 miles*

### Highlights
Tilden Regional Park offers tremendous variety and enjoyment to the visitor. Established in 1936, it is one of the park system's three oldest parks. It was named after Major Charles Lee Tilden, a park founder and the first president of the park district's board of directors. Now dominated by eucalyptus and Monterey pine, the hills were once vast grasslands, with valleys filled by oak, and streams lushly bounded by willow. It is hard to imagine the land without the eucalyptus and pine trees. The landscape, although changed, remains magnificent. Views from the easterly ridges, from Inspiration Point to Vollmer Peak, are spectacular. Several of the promontories in between the two are favorite spots to sit and let gentle breezes chase cares away.

### Getting There
Located just north and east of UC-Berkeley. From Highway 24, east of the Caldecott Tunnel, take the Orinda Village exit. On Camino Pablo, drive through Orinda Village to the intersection with Bear Creek Road to the right and Wildcat Canyon Road to the left. Turn left on Wildcat Canyon Road and drive to Inspiration Point and the parking area. The trailhead for Seaview Trail is approximately 200 yards past Inspiration Point and on the left side of Wildcat Canyon Road.

### The Ride

Ride approximately 2 miles on Wildcat Canyon Road to the trailhead for Seaview Trail to the left. Once on Seaview the fire road climbs somewhat sharply for about .5 mile, passing a junction with Big Springs Trail to the right along the way. The next .5 mile — mostly rolling with a few sharp ascents — brings you to a wonderful picnic table atop an unnamed peak. The view from here is spectacular, looking over Briones Reservoir, San Pablo Reservoir, the Briones Regional Park, and Mount Diablo in the distance. Spend a few minutes here for lunch or a well-deserved break. The next .3 mile drops you quickly to the intersection with Big Springs Trail bearing right. (You have an option of continuing straight on the Skyline Trail to Vollmer Peak, elevation 1,913 feet, approximately .9 mile away. You will, however, have to retrace your steps once there.) On Big Springs the road descends rapidly .6 mile to a parking area on South Park Drive. Of special interest is the annual newt migration that occurs here during rainy weather. During this time, South Park Road may be closed to auto access to protect the little newts. This doesn't affect mountain biking, however, just the auto access via South Park, but don't forget to keep an eye out for them. Cross the parking area and bear right, still on Big Springs. Just past the parking area, bear left on Quarry for a 1.2-mile rolling ride to the Quarry Picnic area and Wildcat Canyon Road and pass another intersection with Big Springs while on Quarry. This trail can be somewhat muddy during wet weather. Turn right on Wildcat Canyon Road and pedal a fairly level .4 mile back to Inspiration Point and the parking area.

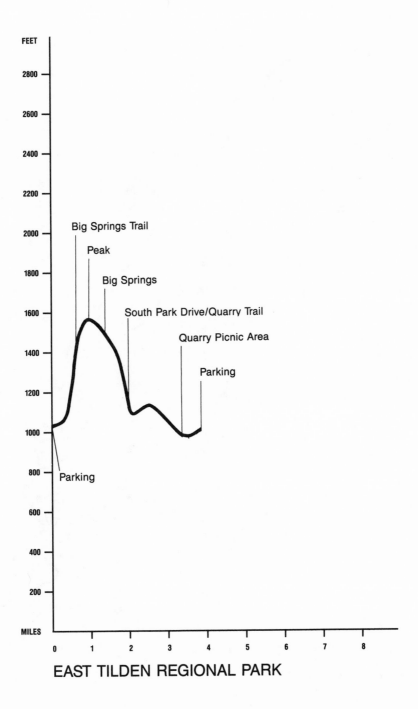

# EAST TILDEN REGIONAL PARK

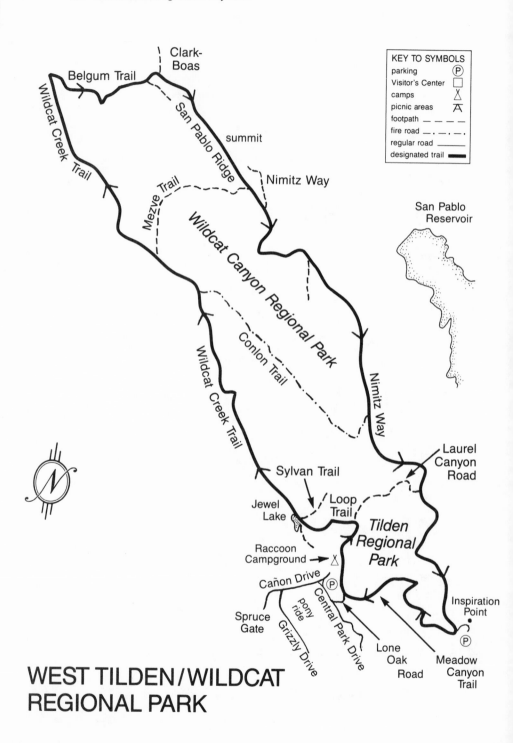

KEY TO SYMBOLS
parking       Ⓟ
Visitor's Center   ☐
camps       ⼈
picnic areas    ⼈
footpath  — — — —
fire road  —.—.—.
regular road  ————
designated trail  ▬▬▬

Clark-Boas

Belgum Trail

Wildcat Creek Trail

San Pablo Ridge

summit

Nimitz Way

Mezve Trail

San Pablo Reservoir

Wildcat Canyon Regional Park

Wildcat Creek Trail

Conlon Trail

Nimitz Way

Sylvan Trail

Laurel Canyon Road

Jewel Lake

Loop Trail

Tilden Regional Park

Raccoon Campground

Cañon Drive

pony ride

Spruce Gate

Grizzly Drive

Central Park Drive

Lone Oak Road

Inspiration Point

Meadow Canyon Trail

N

# WEST TILDEN/WILDCAT REGIONAL PARK

# Chapter Twenty
# WEST TILDEN AND
# WILDCAT REGIONAL PARK

**TRAILHEAD:** *Loop Trail, Raccoon Group Camp*
**TOPO:** *Richmond and Briones Valley*
**OVERALL DIFFICULTY:** *Moderately strenuous*
**TECHNICAL DIFFICULTY:** *Moderate*
**DISTANCE:** *13.3 miles*

### Highlights

Called the "crown jewel" of the East Bay Regional Park system, 2,078-acre Tilden Regional Park is indeed a gem. Established in 1936, it is one of the oldest in the regional park system and offers the visitor a wide range of recreational, environmental, and historical experiences. Tilden was named after Major Charles Lee Tilden, a park founder and the first president of the park district's board of directors. Although hard to imagine, the area, now thick with introduced eucalyptus and Monterey pine, was once a vast grassland with oak-filled valleys.

Largely undeveloped, 2,428-acre Wildcat Regional Park lies adjacent and to the northwest of Tilden. Today, few could guess Wildcat's tumultuous past. Battles over disputed land between Mexican land grant owners, squatters, and speculators occurred between 1870 and 1882. From 1882 to 1920, the battles switched to water rights over Wildcat Canyon's once plentiful streams and springs, ending only when East Bay Municipal Utilities District brought water from the Mokelumne River. During the mid-1960s Standard Oil drilled exploratory wells but luckily found too little to exploit. The area was officially named a park in 1976.

Near the intersection of Wildcat Creek Trail and Belgum Trail along the abandoned road and parking area is a site of additional interest.

135

The cracking and destruction of the road is testament that Wildcat Park straddles the Hayward Fault—reason enough not to encourage development.

In both Tilden and Wildcat, fox, raccoon, skunk, opossum, deer, and ground squirrel dominate the land, while red-tailed hawk, kestrel, sharp-shinned hawk, Cooper's hawk, and turkey vulture can be seen wheeling over head; if you're out for a sunset ride, you may be lucky enough to see or hear a great horned owl. As you pedal along the canyon, the beauty of the area will go unquestioned. A word of caution—as with most Bay Area parks, poison oak is prevalent everywhere.

### Getting There

Located just north and east of UC-Berkeley. From Interstate 80, exit at University Avenue and follow University to Martin Luther King. Turn left on Martin Luther King and drive to Marin. Turn right on Marin and continue until Marin runs into Spruce. Turn left on Spruce and drive until you run into an intersection at Spruce Gate with Grizzly, Wildcat Canyon, and Canon drives. Turn left on Canon Drive. Descend on Canon Drive to Central Park Drive and turn right. Drive past the Pony Rides and turn left on Lone Oak Road to the day-use parking area for the playing field and Lone Oak Picnic area. The Loop Trail trailhead is just up Lone Oak Road at the gated entrance.

### The Ride

To preserve both the environment and your sanity, this ride is best experienced when the trail is relatively dry. We encountered severe mud on one attempt that completely clogged up our bike's derailleurs, forks, chains, you name it, requiring us to hike out carrying our bikes and 40-plus unplanned pounds of mud. It was a unique experience to say the least.

Beginning at the car, ride .2 mile uphill past the Lone Oak Picnic Area to the Raccoon Group Camp and the start of the Loop Trail. Follow the Loop Trail .8 mile to the intersection with Wildcat Creek Trail and Jewel Lake. It is worth stepping off the bikes for a minute here to enjoy the beauty of Jewel Lake. When ready, continue right on the Wildcat Creek Trail to the boundary with Wildcat Regional Park at .9 mile. The dirt road remains relatively flat with a few brief ups and downs for the next 2.3 miles until encountering an abandoned paved road and parking area. Note the impact of the Hayward Fault on this area.

Continue straight for .8 rolling mile until the intersection with Belgum Trail. Bear right on Belgum and begin climbing sharply .9 mile to the junction of Clark Boas and San Pablo Ridge trails. Ignore the unmarked road to the right and continue past the Clark Boas Trail several hundred

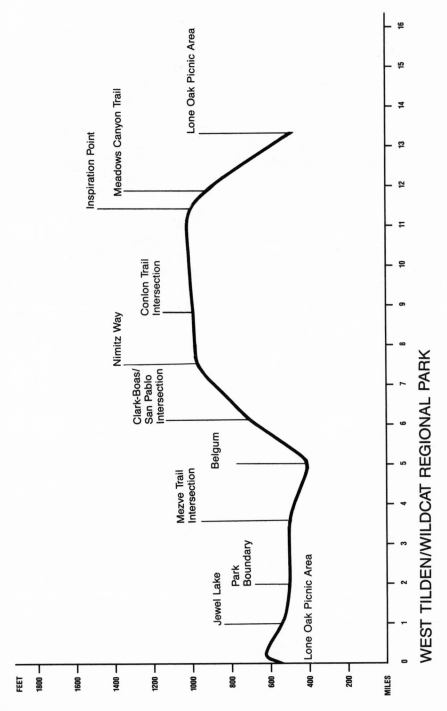

WEST TILDEN/WILDCAT REGIONAL PARK

yards where you will encounter the San Pablo Ridge Trail cutoff to the right. The San Pablo Trail follows the ridgeline over the next 1.3 miles with several very steep uphills and a final downhill past the cutoff to Mezue Trail and the meeting with Nimitz Way .3 mile later. We found an excellent place to enjoy a lunch break and take in the distant views of the Bay, Mount Tamalpais, and Mount Diablo at a high point on the ridge. Once on Nimitz Way there is an option; the 4.2-mile trail to Inspiration Point is paved, gently rolling, and heavily used by hikers, bikers, and equestrians. If you wish to avoid the sometimes crowded (particularly on weekends) conditions, exit on the Conlon Trail — approximately 1.2 miles from the Nimitz and San Pablo Ridge Trail intersection — and descend to Wildcat Creek Trail. Turn left and retrace your path back to the parking area. If you choose to proceed on Nimitz Way, use extra caution; it is easy to pick up excessive speed. Stay in tight control and remember to call out courteously when passing others. Once at Inspiration Point, turn right on Curran Trail and begin descending, now on dirt, .1 mile to the intersection with Meadows Canyon Trail. Head right on Meadows Canyon for a wild and bumpy 1.5-mile descent back to Lone Oak and the parking area.

## Chapter Twenty-One
# MOUNT DIABLO STATE PARK

---

*Ride #1*
**TRAILHEAD:** *Wall Point Road, Rock City Picnic Area*
**TOPO:** *Diablo, Las Trampas Ridge, Walnut Creek, Clayton*
**OVERALL DIFFICULTY:** *Moderate*
**TECHNICAL DIFFICULTY:** *Moderate*
**DISTANCE:** *7.3 miles*

*Ride #2*
**TRAILHEAD:** *Wall Point Road, Rock City Picnic Area*
**TOPO:** *Diablo, Las Trampas Ridge, Walnut Creek, Clayton*
**OVERALL DIFFICULTY:** *Moderately Strenuous*
**TECHNICAL DIFFICULTY:** *Moderate*
**DISTANCE:** *13 miles*

*Ride #3*
**TRAILHEAD:** *Deer Flat Road, Juniper Campground*
**TOPO:** *Clayton*
**OVERALL DIFFICULTY:** *Strenuous*
**TECHNICAL DIFFICULTY:** *Moderate*
**DISTANCE:** *13.3 miles*

*Highlights*
Standing proudly at the eastern edge of the San Francisco Bay Region, Mount Diablo casts an imposing figure, towering 3,849 feet above the surrounding countryside. No other immediate point in the Central Valley or Coast Range is as high, and the view from on top is nothing short of spectacular, especially after a winter storm when the air and horizon are

139

clear. With binoculars you can see west to the Golden Gate Bridge and beyond to the Farallon Islands; southeast is 4,213-foot high Mount Hamilton; looking south you can see Loma Prieta peak in the Santa Cruz Mountains; to the north the world opens with views of Mount Saint Helena in the Coast Range; and on a very clear day, to the east is majestic Half Dome in Yosemite National Park.

In 1851, the peak was used by a survey party as a starting point for surveying the surrounding public domain. After erecting a flagpole at the summit, the members of the survey party extended base and meridian lines that we still use today in official land surveys — legal descriptions of real estate throughout much of California and parts of Oregon and Nevada refer to Mount Diablo base and meridian lines. In 1874 toll roads were opened up to the Mount House, a 16-room hotel near the top of the peak. Celebrities from all over the world visited to enjoy the sunrise, sunset, and occasional full moon from the upper slopes of the mountain.

The summit platform and hotel burned in 1891. Shortly thereafter, the toll roads were closed. The area was used mostly for grazing until 1915, when the toll roads were reopened and public access was restored to the peak. In 1921 a small section of mountain was declared a state park and much of the remaining mountain protected as a game refuge. The state acquired additional land in 1931, and the area was formally dedicated as Mount Diablo State Park.

### Getting There
Located just east of Walnut Creek and Interstate 680. From Interstate 680 take Ygnacio Valley Road through the city of Walnut Creek to an intersection with Walnut Avenue. Turn right on Walnut Avenue and drive to the intersection with Oak Grove Road and turn right; proceed several hundred yards and bear left on North Gate Road. Follow North Gate as it winds and climbs into the park and to the headquarters and the intersection with the Summit Road and South Gate Road.

### The Ride
### Ride #1
Beginning at Wall Point Road trailhead near a maintenance area above Rock City, head in a northerly direction (avoid the trail to the right, which leads to the summit) toward Dan Cook Canyon Trail, .2 mile away. From the intersection with Dan Cook Trail, head straight, remaining on the Wall Point Road. Descend on a sometimes sandy track 2.5 miles, passing Emmons Canyon Road to the left, and continue .6 mile to the intersection of Pine Canyon Trail and Mount Diablo Trail. Turn right and continue descending toward Pine Creek and a gate crossing at .5 mile

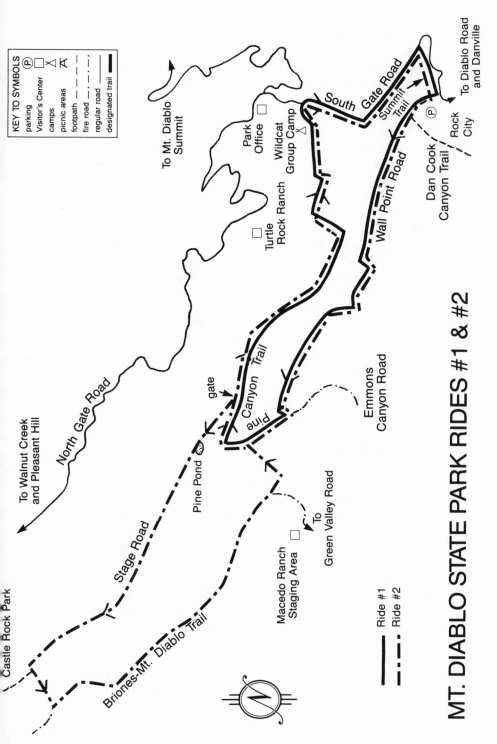

KEY TO SYMBOLS

parking Ⓟ
Visitor's Center ☐
camps △
picnic areas 🛆
footpath ········
fire road —··—··—
regular road —·—·—
designated trail ▬▬▬

To Mt. Diablo
Summit

To Walnut Creek
and Pleasant Hill

North Gate Road

Castle Rock Park

Stage Road

Pine Pond

gate

Pine Canyon Trail

Turtle
Rock Ranch

Park
Office

Wildcat
Group Camp

South Gate Road

Summit
Trail

Wall Point Road

Dan Cook
Canyon Trail

Rock
City Ⓟ

To Diablo Road
and Danville

Emmons
Canyon Road

Macedo Ranch
Staging Area

To
Green Valley Road

Briones-Mt. Diablo Trail

Ride #1
Ride #2

MT. DIABLO STATE PARK RIDES #1 & #2

(Ride #2 description begins here and will bear left).

Turn right at the gate and begin a long and tedious 2.3-mile climb past Wildcat Group Camp to South Gate Road. This section climbs through some beautiful wooded areas and winds past several private roads leading to Turtle Rock Ranch. At the Wildcat Group Camp Trail intersection, pass through the gate, over the cattle crossing, and follow the service road, climbing .2 mile to a right turn on South Gate Road. Traffic on this road can be heavy; beware of vehicles, especially on tight turns. Proceed downhill .9 mile to a large dirt parking area on the right and the Summit Trail. Descend on the Summit Tail .3 mile to Rock City and the parking area.

## Ride #2

Beginning at the gate and the intersection with Pine Canyon and Stage Road in Ride #1, bear left and follow the canyon .4 mile to Pine Pond. From here the road turns somewhat messy in spots as it crosses Pine Creek several times. Continue a lush and beautiful .7 mile to the Mount Diablo Park and Diablo Foothills Regional Park boundary, crossing the muddy and challenging Pine Creek several times. At the boundary, the trail becomes dry again and winds .9 mile along the valley and meadows. To the right is spectacular Castle Rock; on the left you will encounter rock formations before the unsigned intersection near a concrete sluice. To the right takes you toward Castle Rock Park, which at the time of printing is illegal for bikes, although Diablo Park is attempting to acquire access.

Your path takes you left and up .5 mile to the Briones–Mount Diablo Trail. During this short climb keep left when passing through several intersections. At the gate head left on the Briones–Mount Diablo Trail, pedaling a rolling 1.4 miles to another gate; continue .9 mile to an intersection with a road on the right leading out to residential development and Green Valley Road. Head left and up .4 mile to the intersection with Wall Point Road and Pine Canyon Trail. Continue left and down .5 mile on Pine Canyon Trail to a gate and the intersection with Stage Road. At the gate turn right and begin a tedious 2.5-mile climb past Wildcat Group Camp Trail and South Gate Road. Head right on South Gate Road and ride a fast .9-mile descent to a dirt parking area and the Summit Trail connector on the right to Rock City. While on South Gate Road remember to stay alert for RVs and cars barreling around the sharp corners. Descend .3 mile on the Summit Trail to Rock City and your car.

## Ride #3

Beginning at the Juniper Campground day-use parking area, proceed through the campground service road loop to a gate for the trailhead of

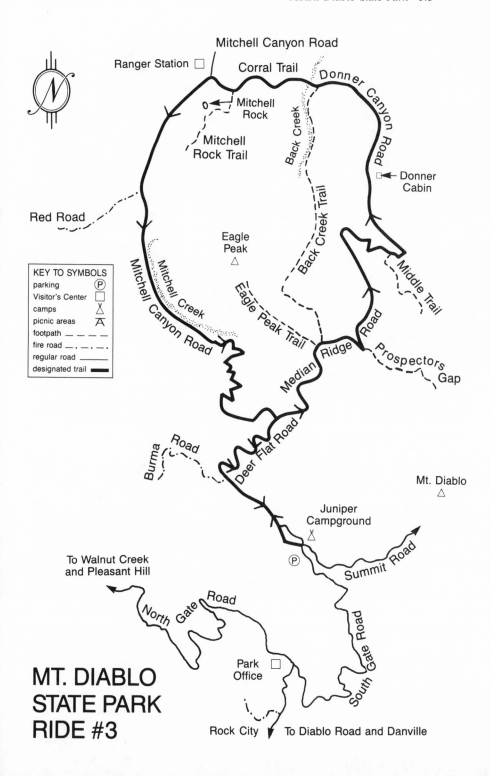

KEY TO SYMBOLS
parking     Ⓟ
Visitor's Center     ☐
camps     ⛺
picnic areas     ⛩
footpath     — — —
fire road     —.—.—.
regular road     ——
designated trail     ▬▬▬

Mitchell Canyon Road

Ranger Station ☐

Corral Trail

Donner Canyon Road

Mitchell Rock

Mitchell Rock Trail

Back Creek

☐ ← Donner Cabin

Red Road

Eagle Peak △

Back Creek Trail

Middle Trail

Mitchell Creek

Mitchell Canyon Road

Eagle Peak Trail

Median Ridge Road

Prospectors Gap

Burma Road

Deer Flat Road

Mt. Diablo △

Juniper Campground ⛺

To Walnut Creek and Pleasant Hill

Ⓟ

Summit Road

North Gate Road

Park Office ☐

South Gate Road

Rock City ▼    To Diablo Road and Danville

# MT. DIABLO STATE PARK RIDE #3

Deer Flat Road. The next .7 mile is a moderate descent to the inter-section with Burma Road. Continue straight to Deer Flat; this 1.1-mile section is quite steep, rutted, and occasionally loose. Stay in control and enjoy! At Deer Flat, bear right and begin the brief but steep climb on Median Ridge Road, passing the intersection with Eagle Peak Trail at .8 mile. Remain on Median Ridge Road .4 mile to the intersection with Prospectors Gap Road and hang a sharp left for a bone-jarring 1.5-mile descent to the intersection with Donner Canyon Road. Donner Canyon Road bears left for a scenic 1.8-mile pedal through the canyon past the site of Donner Cabin.

Upon leaving the canyon, join the Corral Trail for a rolling and open 1.2 miles to Mitchell Canyon Road. This area is somewhat confusing, but it is helpful to keep the quarry on the right, while skirting the base of the hills to the left. At the ranger station turn left on Mitchell Canyon Road and begin the gentle climb along Mitchell Creek. At approximately 1.8 miles there is a wonderful open grassy area that is a great location for a rest and a bite to eat before the steep climb. The next 2.2-mile stretch to Deer Flat is a tedious but manageable climb. Despite the specter of the ridge looming above, numerous switchbacks and a steady incline help to make the climb tolerable. At Deer Flat, retrace your path back up Deer Flat Road 1.8 miles to Juniper Campground and the parking area.

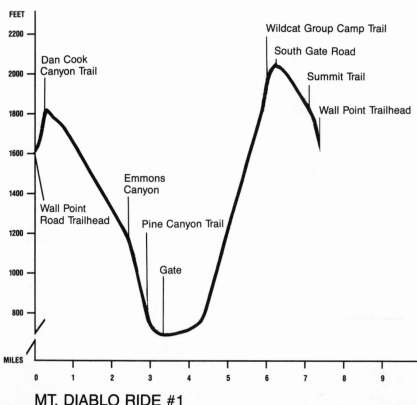

MT. DIABLO RIDE #1

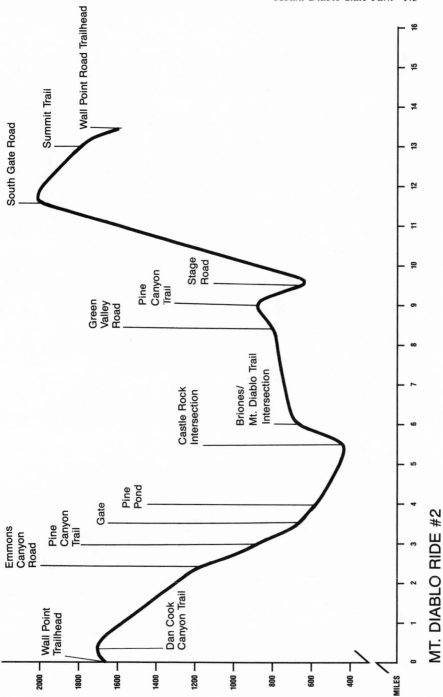

MT. DIABLO RIDE #2

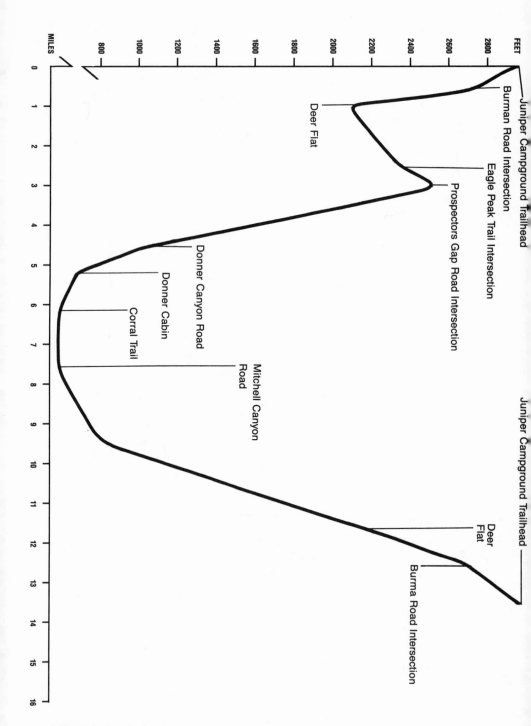

MT. DIABLO RIDE #3

## Chapter Twenty-Two
# GOLDEN GATE NATIONAL RECREATION AREA

**TRAILHEAD:** *Miwok*
**TOPO:** *Point Bonita*
**OVERALL DIFFICULTY:** *Moderate*
**TECHNICAL DIFFICULTY:** *Easy/Moderate*
**DISTANCE:** *6.8 miles*

### GGNRA — South
#### *Highlights*
The Golden Gate National Recreation Area is a massive expanse of land set aside to preserve some of San Francisco Bay's most spectacular natural landmarks. The area was dedicated in 1983 by Congress to the memory of San Franciscan Representative Philip Burton, a leader in conservation and park issues while in office. Regulated by the National Park Service, the park extends to both the north and south of the Golden Gate Bridge, although our rides only encompass the northern region.

The GGNRA tempts the visitor with a little of everything. Redwood forests, secluded beaches, rugged shorelines, inland lakes, tumbling streams, and grassy hilltops provide an awe-inspiring escape from the confines of the nearby city. Don't be surprised by the solitude you will find, or the crowds evident near the most accessible areas. If you begin early in the morning and are quiet, you will probably be afforded wondrous glimpses of wildlife such as deer, bobcats, numerous hawks, raccoons, and, in late fall and early spring, migrating whales.

A word of advice: bring several layers of clothing. Many of the ridges in the GGNRA are exposed and extremely windswept. Early morning fog can be quite dense, swirling, and damp and, unless you are dressed

147

## GGNRA North

Ride #1 ━━━━━
Ride #2 ▪━▪━▪

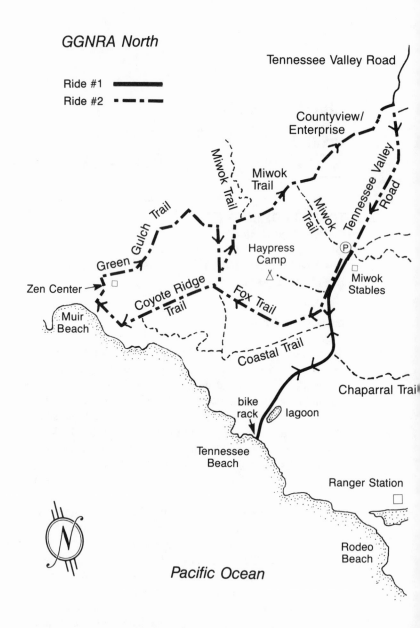

Tennessee Valley Road

Countyview/
Enterprise

Miwok Trail

Miwok Trail

Miwok Trail

Tennessee Valley Road

Green Gulch Trail

Zen Center

Haypress Camp

Coyote Ridge Trail

Fox Trail

Ⓟ

Miwok Stables

Muir Beach

Coastal Trail

Chaparral Trail

bike rack

lagoon

Tennessee Beach

Ranger Station

Rodeo Beach

Pacific Ocean

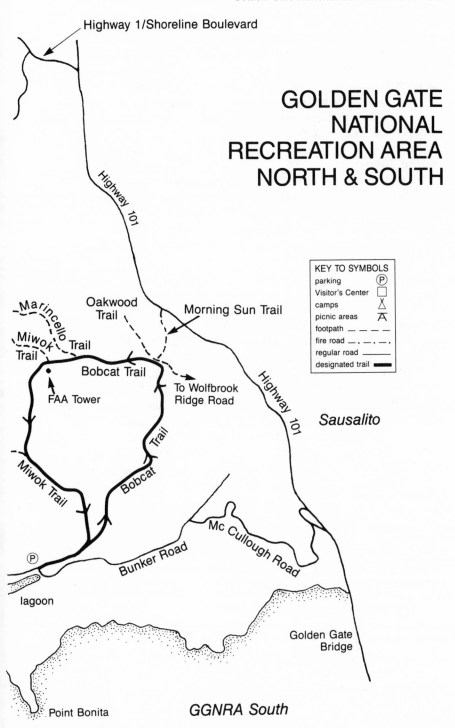

Highway 1/Shoreline Boulevard

# GOLDEN GATE NATIONAL RECREATION AREA NORTH & SOUTH

Highway 101

KEY TO SYMBOLS
parking ⓟ
Visitor's Center ☐
camps 𝝙
picnic areas 𝚨
footpath _ _ _ _
fire road _ . _ . _ .
regular road _____
designated trail ▬▬▬

Marincello Trail

Oakwood Trail

Morning Sun Trail

Miwok Trail

Bobcat Trail

FAA Tower

To Wolfbrook Ridge Road

Highway 101

*Sausalito*

Bobcat Trail

Miwok Trail

Mc Cullough Road

ⓟ

Bunker Road

lagoon

Golden Gate Bridge

Point Bonita

*GGNRA South*

for it, can cut right to the bone; conversely, inland canyons can be solar ovens, leaving you dry and shriveled like a raisin. Dress appropriately for all of Marin's moods and you will experience an environment that is unique and spectacular at anytime. (*Note: As of June 1992, all rides described are, to the best of our knowledge, legal; however, due to possible impending changes, riders should inquire about current trail status at GGNRA office at 415-331-1540.*)

### Getting There
From Interstate 101 just north of the Golden Gate Bridge, exit on Alexander Road and head west. Bear right on McCullough Road to another left on Bunker Road. Continue to the ranger station across from Rodeo Beach and Lagoon. There is parking here or you can return approximately .5 mile to a large dirt parking area in front of a large one-story building and the trailhead for Miwok Trail.

### The Ride
The Miwok Trail begins just past the gate near the parking area. Pedal .4 mile to the intersection and bear right onto Bobcat Trail. Continue 2 miles steadily up until it levels and intersects with Oakwood Trail (illegal for mountain bikes). Stay left on Bobcat .8 mile to the intersection with Marincello Trail to the right (Marincello descends approximately 1.3 miles to the Tennessee Valley Road). Continue straight .3 mile to the Miwok Trail (south), which bears to the right. There is an FAA flight transmitter at the top of the peak here—well worth a lunch stop to enjoy views of Sausalito, Napa Valley, and San Francisco Bay and the San Francisco skyline. Miwok Trail winds and descends 1.4 miles to the intersection with Bobcat Trail bearing to the left; continue .4 mile to right and the Miwok Trail parking area.

### GGNRA—North
**TRAILHEAD:** *Tennessee Valley Trail to Tennessee Beach*

**Ride #1**
**TOPO:** *Point Bonita*
**OVERALL DIFFICULTY:** *Easy*
**TECHNICAL DIFFICULTY:** *Easy*
**DISTANCE:** *Approximately 3.8 miles round-trip*

**Ride #2**
**TOPO:** *Point Bonita and San Rafael*
**OVERALL DIFFICULTY:** *Moderate/Difficult*
**TECHNICAL DIFFICULTY:** *Moderate*
**DISTANCE:** *Approximately 9.7 miles*

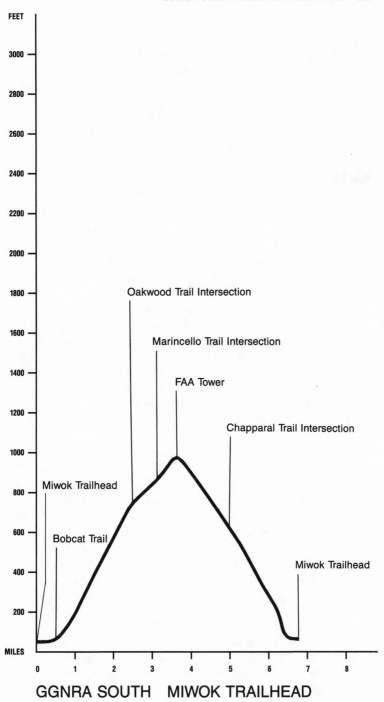

**GGNRA SOUTH   MIWOK TRAILHEAD**

### Getting There

From Interstate 101 north of the Golden Gate Bridge take the Highway 1/Shoreline Avenue exit (north of Sausalito). Head north on Highway 1 toward Muir Beach (well worth a visit). Bear left on Tennessee Valley Road and continue until the dead end and the parking area by Miwok Stables. This parking area can be very crowded on weekends, as Tennessee Beach is a very popular site to visit. Get an early start to beat the crowds — 7 A.M. isn't as ridiculous as it sounds!

### Ride #1

This is an outstanding beginner ride with little difficulty except perhaps the final hill near the beach. From Miwok Stables and the parking area pedal .3 mile to the trail to Haypress Camp branching off to the right. Haypress Camp is a .5-mile pedal off the Tennessee Valley Trail and nestled in a grove of eucalyptus trees. The camp is secluded and comes equipped with an outhouse, picnic tables, and several campsites. For campground reservations here or anywhere else in the GGNRA, call 415-331-1540. Continue straight .1 mile to Fox Trail, also branching off to the right (Ride #2 description heading up Fox Trail begins here). Continuing straight, the road will turn from paved to hard-pack dirt. Approximately .5 mile from Fox you will cross the intersection with Coastal Trail bearing right and up to Coyote Ridge. Your road takes you straight and approximately 1 mile to Tennessee Beach. There is a bike rack here, so take advantage of the opportunity to secure your bike and enjoy the scenery. Return the way you came.

### Ride #2

*Read description for Ride #1 from the parking area to the intersection of Fox Trail and Tennessee Valley road.* Climb steadily up Fox Trail to the intersection with Coyote Ridge Trail branching left and right. You will continue pedaling uphill a short distance on a section where both Coyote and Fox share the same road. Coyote will head off to the left, through a gate, and continue across the ridgeline. Your path will continue straight and descend to the intersection with Coastal Trail.

Coastal (illegal for mountain bikes) is a single track hugging the coast and forking off to the left. Stop and listen to the pounding surf several hundred feet below you. The loss in elevation from here to Muir Beach is rapid, rocky, and rutted, so stay in control. At the bottom of the hill, you can either bear right and join up with Green Gulch Trail or bear left for a view of Muir Beach and a little sunbathing. Either way, you will eventually want to be pedaling your bike along Green Gulch. You will pass through several gates and be on the property of the Zen Center Farm

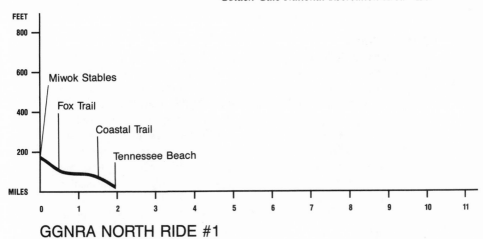

**GGNRA NORTH RIDE #1**

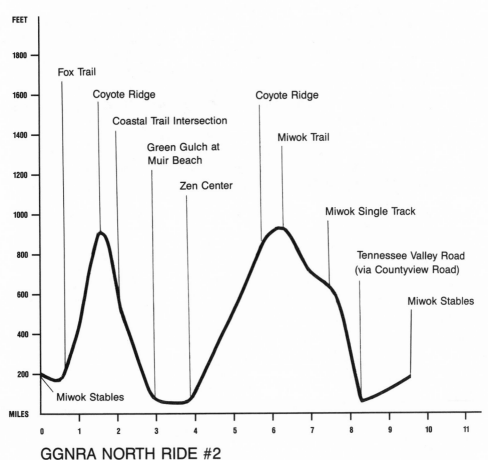

**GGNRA NORTH RIDE #2**

for the first .5 mile or so of Green Gulch. Please close all gates behind you, ride slowly and quietly, and respect the Zen Center's desire for privacy.

Once you begin riding on paved road, keep a careful eye out for Green Gulch switching back and uphill to the right. Everything is well signed, but the signs are small and easily missed. At the switchback, you will begin to experience the "Zen" of riding uphill through loose rutted trail — for what seems an eternity. You will pass by a small cabin overlooking the valley below. This cabin is kept by the Zen Center and is private. Ride slow and steady and you will eventually reach the intersection with Coyote Ridge Trail. Head left for a wonderful ride along the ridge with spectacular views east and west.

At the intersection of Coyote Ridge and Miwok bear left and continue downhill on Miwok. This section of Miwok affords the rider a magical descent through a dense stand of Eucalyptus trees. Miwok gets somewhat confusing at the bottom of the hill, as it leaves the grove of trees. The first intersection is Miwok heading left and right. Go right and uphill away from Marin Drive to an open area and several trails merging together. Several trails, one of which is Miwok, branch off to the right and downhill to the parking area. These are single track and illegal for bicycles. Your path will take you straight and out to Countyview Drive. The remaining section of the ride will take you back to the parking area by road — remember that you are now in the presence of cars. Countyview turns into Enterprise Concourse, which you will follow until meeting up with Tennessee Valley Road. Turn right and pedal about 1.2 miles back up to the parking area and your car. Whew!

## Chapter Twenty-Three

# MOUNT TAMALPAIS

### *Highlights*

Officially designated a state park in 1931, Mount Tamalpais is the center attraction for one of the most visited and popular areas for mountain bikers. A potential mountain biker's paradise, Mount Tamalpais State Park encompasses more than 6,000 acres with many fire roads that are legal and suitable for mountain bikes. In addition to this massive expanse of land, neighboring Marin Municipal Water District is the sole proprietor of the property surrounding Mount Tamalpais.

Yet all is not well with the mountain biking situation at Mount Tamalpais. The area is also a favorite stomping ground for numerous equestrians, hikers, wanderers, nature lovers, and others—and no wonder, the views and rugged terrain of the area are spectacular. Herein the lies the problem: Where do you draw the line and limit or control use of the park? The controversy continues to boil, causing some ridiculous and ugly encounters. While researching this book, we heard numerous reports of verbal and physical confrontations between mountain bikers, hikers, equestrians, and rangers that recall the range wars of the old West (sans Winchester rifles of course!).

Rangers in the Mount Tamalpais area have had to resort to setting up radar-gun checkpoints and handing out hefty tickets to those mountain bikers exceeding 15 mph—not a hard speed to exceed by any stretch of the imagination. The Marin Municipal Water District is considering placing serious restrictions on the use of their roads and the closure of many others.

At the very root of these strict regulations is the problem of overuse and lack of communication and education at all levels—hikers, equestrians, mountain bikers, and law enforcement officers alike. At the time of going to press, no immediate or long-range solution seemed in place. Because of this we felt that it was in our reader's best interest, and the best interest of the area, not to describe rides in detail. We have included brief descriptions of some of the more popular rides for your benefit, since this is potentially a wonderful location to ride—however, there are other areas described in this book that we feel are just as memorable, less populated, and easily accessible for your riding pleasure.

If you wish a more detailed description of the Mount Tamalpais area, we recommend *The Marin Mountain Bike Guide* by Armor Todd, available in most Marin County bike shops.

### Getting There

Located just north of the Golden Gate Bridge and east of Highway 101 and Marin. From Highway 101 take the Panoramic Highway/Highway 1 to The Mountain Home Inn. This is a very good central parking area for bike exploration. Farther along Highway 1 there is a ranger station at Pantoll, where they will have more information about trail accessibility and additional trailhead parking.

### Railroad Grade

Set on the route of the once famous Mount Tamalpais Scenic Railway, Old Railroad Grade continues to be one of the most popular bike routes in the park. Beginning at West Blithedale Road (just off Tiburon Boulevard) the route climbs steadily but gently approximately 7 miles to the top of Mount Tamalpais. Along the way you will encounter superb views; one of the most spectacular is from the veranda of West Point Inn, while sipping lemonade. West Point Inn is operated by a volunteer organization and serves coffee, tea, lemonade, and snacks for a small donation. There are even rooms upstairs for an overnight stay if you wish; check with the Inn at 415-388-9955 for reservation information.

### Old Stage Road

A fairly easy connecting route from the Pantoll parking area to West Point Inn. Once used as a stagecoach route, the Old Stage Road provides beginners with an excellent opportunity to enjoy Mount Tamalpais. From West Point Inn, the Old Stage Road serves as an easy escape to the surrounding headlands and down to Muir Beach—remember though, whatever you descend you will have to climb later in the day.

### Hoo-Koo-E-Koo

Named after the Native American tribe that once resided in the area, the route, though somewhat rocky, requires a certain amount of technical expertise. It is, however, an excellent traverse from Old Railroad Grade just above Double Bow Knot to the Marin Lakes area from on top of Blithedale Ridge.

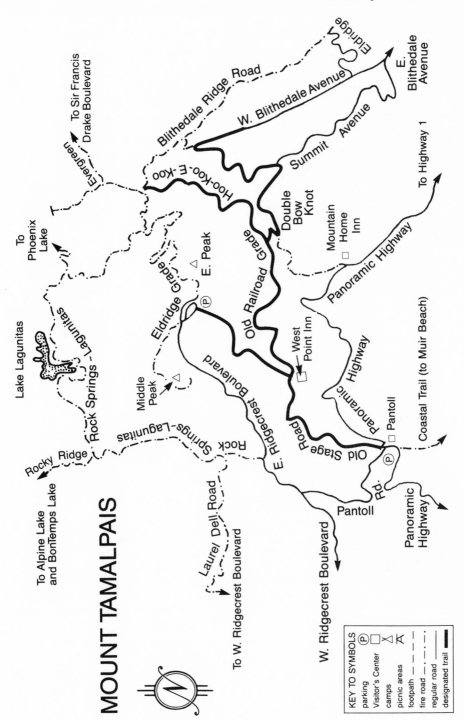

MOUNT TAMALPAIS

KEY TO SYMBOLS
parking ⓟ
Visitor's Center ☐
camps ⚐
picnic areas ⋔
footpath — — —
fire road —··—··—
regular road
designated trail ▬▬▬

## Chapter Twenty-Four
# BOLINAS RIDGE

**TRAILHEAD ONE-WAY WITH CAR SHUTTLE:** *Bolinas Ridge Fire Road, Bolinas-Fairfax Road*
**TRAILHEAD ROUND-TRIP:** *Bolinas Ridge Fire Road, Sir Francis Drake Boulevard*
**TOPO:** *Inverness, San Geronimo, Bolinas*
**SPECIAL RIDE INFORMATION:** *Sometimes access is limited due to fire closure, therefore this ride is best enjoyed fall through spring. Call Marin Municipal Water District Ranger Station at 415-459-5267 for information.*
**OVERALL DIFFICULTY:** *One-Way—Moderate; Round-Trip—Strenuous*
**TECHNICAL DIFFICULTY:** *One-way—Moderate; Round-Trip—Moderate*
**DISTANCE:** *Approximately 11.2 miles each way*

### Highlights
This is perhaps the most varied and spectacular ride in Marin county. Bolinas Ridge Fire Road offers the rider exalting downhills; a few gut-wrenching uphills (providing you are riding one way from Bolinas-Fairfax Road to Olema; otherwise the round trip will offer the ultimate in 11.2 miles of thigh-burning uphill); mystical and deeply shadowed redwood groves; and incredible views east to Napa, south to Bolinas Lagoon, west to the hills of Point Reyes, and north to Tomales Bay. The road is hard-packed (provided it hasn't rained recently) and sometimes heavily used by equestrians, runners, hikers, and especially mountain bikers, so stay in control! There are also several cattle gates along the way; remember to close them and watch out for cattle when riding. Enjoy—we think you'll find that this is truly an outstanding ride.

The following are Marin Municipal Water District's bicycle regulations:

BICYCLES: No person shall possess or operate any bicycle or similar vehicle on District lands except upon public roads, parking lots, or protection roads not signed against such use. Use may be restricted or prohibited on any or all roads at the District's discretion. No bicycle or similar vehicle shall be operated in a manner to endanger or frighten hikers, equestrians or others using District lands. Any bicycle or similar vehicle used in violation of these regulations may be impounded.

SPEED LIMITS: Maximum speed limit for all vehicles is 15 miles per hour, unless otherwise posted; however, speeds shall be reduced as conditions warrant. Bicycles are required to slow to 5 miles per hour when passing others using District lands or approaching blind turns. In no case shall a person operate any vehicle, including bicycles, at a speed greater than is reasonable or prudent for safe operation or to protect the safety of others using District lands.

### Getting There
From Highway 101 at the Golden Gate Bridge, drive north to the Sir Francis Drake Boulevard (just south of 580) exit and head west.

### One-way Ride With Car Shuttle
From 101 take Sir Francis Drake Boulevard past Samuel P. Taylor State Park to a dirt parking area on the left side of the road approximately 1 mile before Olema and park one car here. The other vehicle will be parked at the trail head on Bolinas-Fairfax Road; from Sir Francis Drake Boulevard, turn left on Highway 1 at Olema. Drive approximately 9.5 miles to an unsigned left turn, just before Bolinas Lagoon and after Olema-Bolinas Road to the right. Climb a very windy 4.6 miles to the intersection and parking area for Bolinas Ridge Fire Road.

### Round-trip Ride With No Car Shuttle
Park at either end. We recommend beginning at the parking area on Sir Francis Drake Boulevard, just east of Olema. Your ride will then be mostly uphill there and downhill for the return. If you wish to begin your ride from Bolinas Ridge Fire Road Trailhead on Old Bolinas-Fairfax Road, see driving directions below.

On Sir Francis Drake Boulevard, pass through the towns of Kentfield, Ross, and San Anselmo to the town of Fairfax and turn left on Old Bolinas-Fairfax Road. Continue on this road, passing by Meadow Club Golf Course and Alpine Lake. The intersection and parking areas for Bolinas Ridge Fire Road are at the top of a winding grade, approximately 10.7 miles from Sir Francis Drake Boulevard.

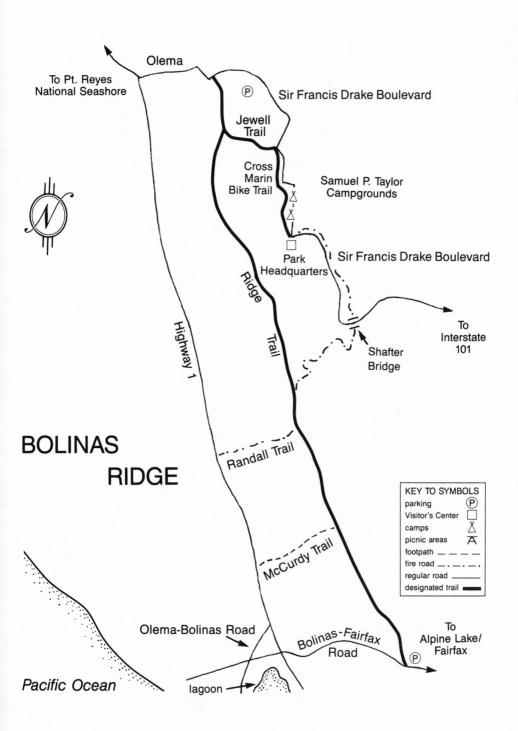

Olema

To Pt. Reyes
National Seashore

Sir Francis Drake Boulevard

Jewell
Trail

Cross
Marin
Bike Trail

Samuel P. Taylor
Campgrounds

Park
Headquarters

Sir Francis Drake Boulevard

To
Interstate
101

Shafter
Bridge

Ridge
Trail

Highway 1

BOLINAS
RIDGE

Randall Trail

McCurdy Trail

KEY TO SYMBOLS
parking                    Ⓟ
Visitor's Center        ☐
camps                      ⋏
picnic areas            ⩚
footpath          _ _ _ _
fire road         _._._.
regular road   _____
designated trail ▬▬▬

Olema-Bolinas Road

Bolinas-Fairfax
Road

To
Alpine Lake/
Fairfax

Pacific Ocean

lagoon →

### The Ride

Pass through the gate and begin your ride at the Bolinas Ridge Fire Road Trailhead on the north side of Bolinas-Fairfax Road. For the first 3.5 miles the trail follows rolling (some steep ascents) terrain through beautiful redwoods. At approximately 3.5 miles you will come to the intersection with McCurdy Trail branching off to the left. Continue straight, descending on the Bolinas Ridge Fire Road, picking your way carefully through exposed tree roots and ruts. Approximately 1.6 miles past McCurdy Trail is the Randall Trail branching off to the left. Continue straight and down, passing the cutoff to Shafter Bridge on the right. Near this point, the terrain opens into rolling grassland and the first of several cattle gates. Please be sure to secure all gates behind you. There is a rock outcropping at this first gate, an ideal spot for lunch and taking in the views of Point Reyes and Tomales Bay in the distance. From here descend to the intersection with Jewell Trail branching off to the right. (Jewell Trail will take you back to Samuel P. Taylor State Park if you are camping there.) Bolinas Ridge Fire Road takes a sharp turn here and continues to the parking area and your second car.

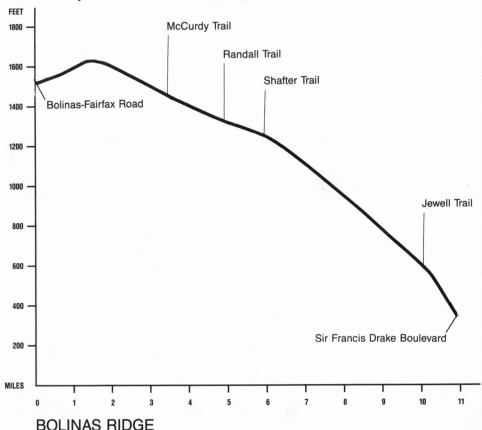

BOLINAS RIDGE

# Chapter Twenty-Five
# SAMUEL P. TAYLOR STATE PARK

**TRAILHEAD:** *Samuel P. Taylor State Park Redwood Grove Picnic Area*
**TOPO:** *San Geronimo*

**Ride #1**
**OVERALL DIFFICULTY:** *Strenuous*
**TECHNICAL DIFFICULTY:** *Moderate*
**DISTANCE:** *Approximately 7 miles*

**Ride #2**
**OVERALL DIFFICULTY:** *Easy*
**TECHNICAL DIFFICULTY:** *Easy*
**DISTANCE:** *Approximately 6.4 miles*

### Highlights
Located in the steep rolling hills of Marin County, Samuel P. Taylor State Park is an ideal base camp for experiencing some of the finest mountain biking in the north bay. The terrain varies from shady, cool creek beds canopied by towering redwoods to dry and open ridge tops with sweeping views of Tomales Bay and Point Reyes. We recommend exploring for at least a day or two if you wish to truly experience the area's treasures. This will give you ample opportunity to spend some time on Barnabe Peak admiring the inspiring view to the coast or to take a refreshing dip and bask on a rock at one of Papermill Creek's swimming holes.

In the late 1870s, the park's namesake once operated a paper mill (hence the name Papermill Creek) that supplied San Francisco with material for its daily paper; he also dallied in the manufacture of blasting powder until a rather explosive mishap brought this business venture to a close. Taylor

163

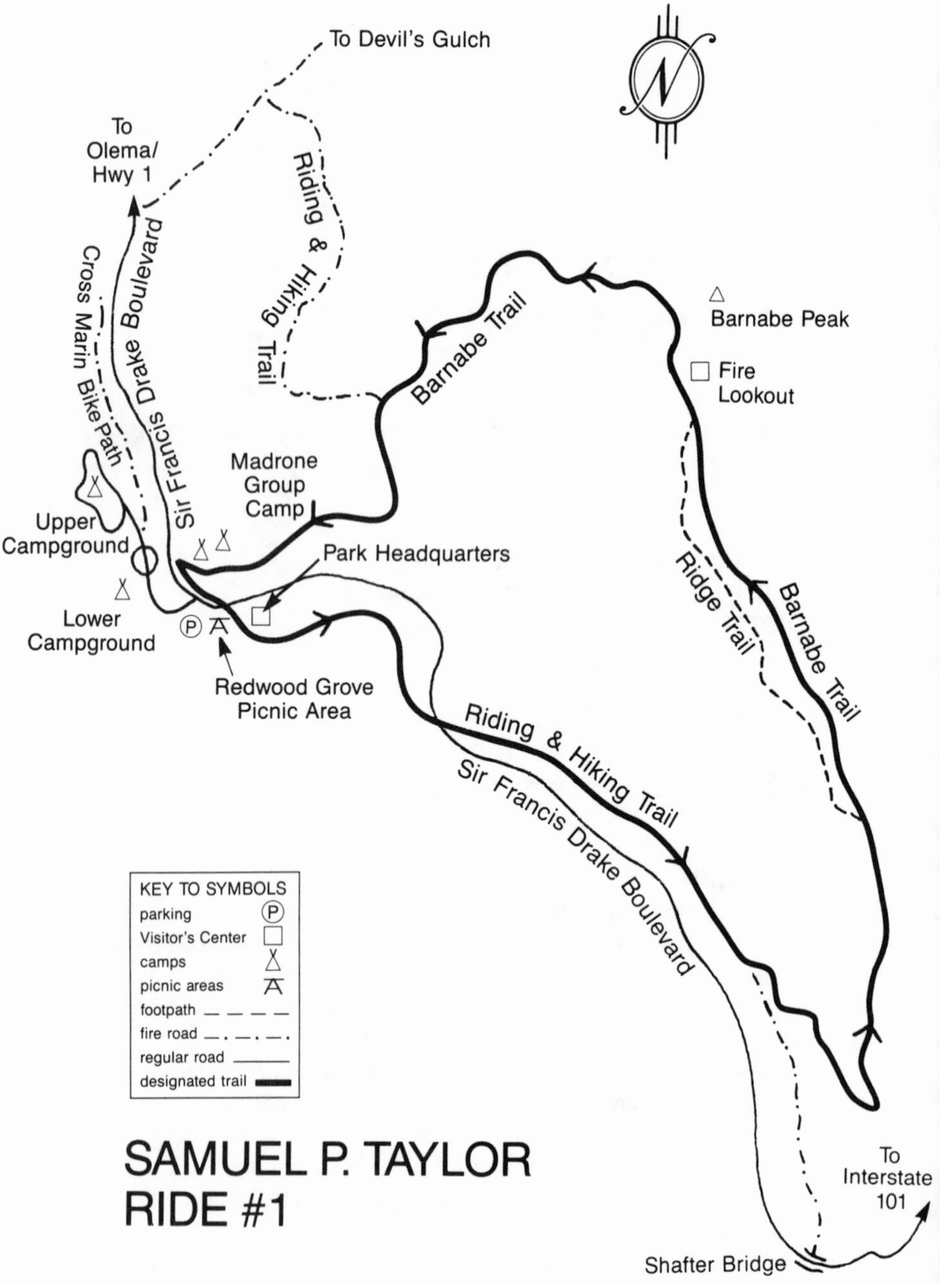

To Devil's Gulch

To Olema/ Hwy 1

Cross Marin Bike Path

Sir Francis Drake Boulevard

Riding & Hiking Trail

Barnabe Trail

△ Barnabe Peak

☐ Fire Lookout

Madrone Group Camp

Ridge Trail

Barnabe Trail

Upper Campground

Park Headquarters

Lower Campground

Redwood Grove Picnic Area

Riding & Hiking Trail

Sir Francis Drake Boulevard

KEY TO SYMBOLS
parking                  Ⓟ
Visitor's Center         ☐
camps                    ⋏
picnic areas             ⊼
footpath         _ _ _ _
fire road        _ . _ . _ .
regular road     _____
designated trail ▬▬▬

To Interstate 101

Shafter Bridge

# SAMUEL P. TAYLOR RIDE #1

# SAMUEL P. TAYLOR STATE PARK RIDE #2

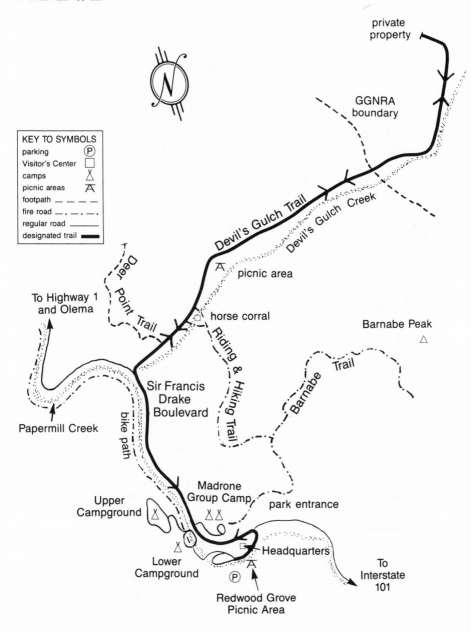

KEY TO SYMBOLS
parking     Ⓟ
Visitor's Center □
camps     ⋏
picnic areas     🛆
footpath _ _ _ _
fire road _.._.._.
regular road _____
designated trail ▬▬▬

private property

GGNRA boundary

Devil's Gulch Trail

Devil's Gulch Creek

Deer Point Trail

To Highway 1 and Olema

picnic area

horse corral

Barnabe Peak △

Riding & Hiking Trail

Barnabe Trail

Sir Francis Drake Boulevard

Papermill Creek

bike path

Madrone Group Camp

park entrance

Upper Campground

Lower Campground

Ⓟ

Redwood Grove Picnic Area

Headquarters

To Interstate 101

later opened a camp and resort hotel beside the newly built narrow-gauge railroad; this was one of the first areas in the United States to offer camping as an outdoor recreation and became one of northern California's most popular weekend play areas.

### Getting There
From Interstate 101 north of the Golden Gate Bridge take the Sir Francis Drake Boulevard exit. Go west on Sir Francis Drake, following the signs for Point Reyes and Samuel P. Taylor State Park. Turn left into the entrance for Samuel P. Taylor State Park and leave your car in the picnic area parking.

### Ride #1
Beginning at the Redwood Grove picnic area past the silver gate, pedal .9 mile to the bridge crossing Sir Francis Drake (parking is also available here if you wish to start your ride from the highway and not from the state park). Continue straight approximately 1.7 miles to a fork where the road to Barnabe Peak heads up and left and the Riding and Hiking Trail heads straight. You will bear left and up, and up, and up, and up—climbing from 200 to more than 1,000 feet in just under 2 miles to the intersection with the single-track Ridge Trail. The Ridge Trail goes left and west, but you will continue to pedal straight and up some more—though somewhat gradually (our thighs were burning by now, how about yours?).

Near the top of Barnabe Peak, and in sight of the Fire Lookout, you will pass through a short section of private land. Respect the privacy and exit almost immediately left at the first gate for a wonderful descent down Barnabe Road and back to the park headquarters. Descend 1.3 miles to the Riding and Hiking Trail intersection and a sharp left turn. Straight will take you to Devil's Gulch. Go left on the Riding and Hiking Trail .8 mile to the Madrone Group Camp. Return to the parking area by heading left on Sir Francis Drake Boulevard.

### Ride #2
Beginning at the Redwood Grove picnic area, pedal approximately .8 mile. Turn left onto Sir Francis Drake Boulevard to a parking area and a right turn onto Devil's Gulch Trail. Pedal steadily up .2 mile to the intersection with Deer Point Trail branching off to the left. There are picnic tables here and a horse corral for equestrian use. Pedal another .1 mile to the intersection with the Riding and Hiking Trail branching off to the right. Continue straight up the road. At this point Devil's Gulch turns to dirt and continues straight up the valley. Ride through beautiful wooded terrain and gently up 1.1 miles to a gate and the state park boundary. Pass through the gate and onto Golden Gate National Recreation Area property.

The trail continues climbing ever so slightly, snaking through the valley and across several beautiful meadows. One mile from the state park boundary, you will encounter a wooden gate that may be open or closed. There are piles of wood, some abandoned cars, etc. From here on is private property, and there is no trespassing. Please respect the privacy of the owner. Turn back and coast virtually all the way to the intersection with the Riding and Hiking Trail. Here you have a choice: either retrace your route completely back to Sir Francis Drake and the park headquarters or bear left on the Riding and Hiking Trail 1.4 miles to the Madrone Group Camp and then out onto Sir Francis Drake and the park headquarters.

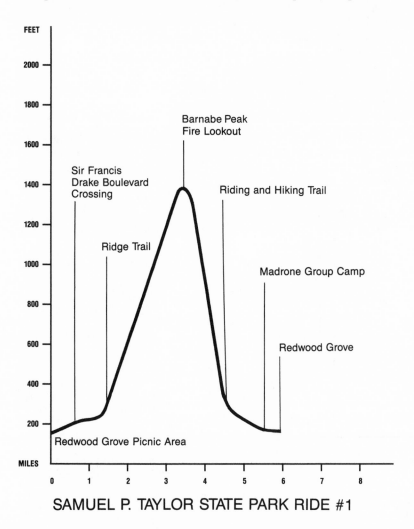

SAMUEL P. TAYLOR STATE PARK RIDE #1

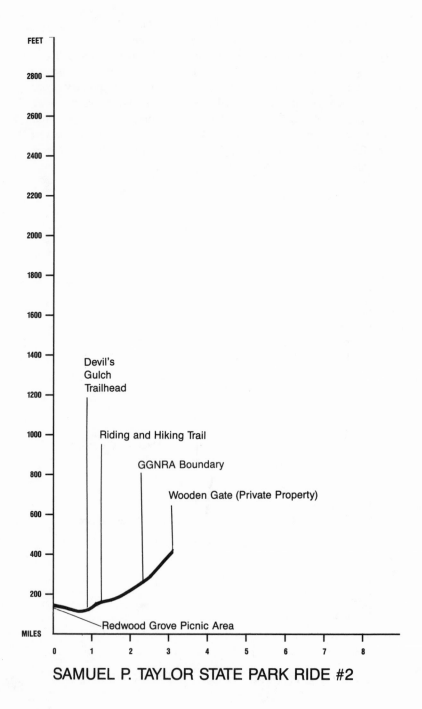

SAMUEL P. TAYLOR STATE PARK RIDE #2

# Chapter Twenty-Six

# POINT REYES

*Ride #1*
**TRAILHEAD:** *Bear Valley and Rift Zone Trail*
**TOPO:** *Inverness and Double Point*
**OVERALL DIFFICULTY:** *Easy*
**TECHNICAL DIFFICULTY:** *Easy*
**DISTANCE:** *Approximately 6.2 miles*

*Ride #2*
**TRAILHEAD:** *Five Brooks*
**TOPO:** *Inverness, Double Point, Bolinas, San Geronimo*
**OVERALL DIFFICULTY:** *Strenuous*
**TECHNICAL DIFFICULTY:** *Moderately Difficult*
**DISTANCE:** *Approximately 19 miles*

## Highlights

Point Reyes National Seashore is an area that abounds with unique geological and natural phenomena. The area rides precariously on the eastern edge of the Pacific plate, which accounts for the fact that the rocks in Point Reyes match those of the Tehachapi Mountains 310 miles to the south. A "belt" of topographic changes and distinct features follow the San Andreas Fault, which runs up the Olema Valley, near park headquarters. In the great earthquake of 1906, the peninsula, hinging upon the Olema Valley, was moved forcefully 20 feet northwestward.

In the spring, mild weather and carpets of wild flowers grace the folded landscape. There are miles of beaches and Douglas fir and Bishop pine forests that stretch to the ocean. During the winter months it is possible to view migrating gray whales just offshore; often the beaches and bays

169

are filled with seals and a wide variety of shore birds. Take your binoculars and enjoy.

There is quite a varied history to be found in this land as well. First inhabited by the Coast Miwok Indians, the area was hunted and harvested peacefully. During the summer of 1579 Sir Francis Drake, an English adventurer, landed here and claimed this land for England and Queen Elizabeth. The English never came back to defend their claim, instead leaving it for the Spaniards to colonize in 1769; during this period, the Miwok Indians had all but been removed from their native land to labor in Spanish missions, and Point Reyes was inhabited by the Miwoks no longer.

Word of the richness of pelts and resources of the area reached many distant nations. This wide influence from the outside world upon the settlers of California and Mexico in part led them to revolt against Spain and establish an independent Republic of Mexico in 1821. The United States takeover of California led to a breakup of large land holdings into numerous cattle ranches. Beef and dairy cattle have wandered Point Reyes ever since. Congress passed legislation protecting Point Reyes as a National Seashore on September 13, 1962.

Within the boundaries there is no car camping. However, there are four hike-in campgrounds available without charge at Bear Valley Visitor Center.

### Getting There

Take the Sir Francis Drake exit off 101 just south of the intersection of Interstate 580 and Highway 101 and north of the Golden Gate Bridge. Travel east on Sir Francis Drake, passing through the towns of Kentfield and Fairfax, past Samuel P. Taylor State Park (a great place to base camp if you are staying overnight; another great camping area is to the east of Pt. Reyes), to Olema and the intersection with Highway 1. Turn right on Highway 1 and bear left almost immediately on Bear Valley Road. There is a mountain bike rental shop on the corner here called Trail Head Rentals. Its number is 415-663-1958. Once on Bear Valley Road travel about .5 mile to the park headquarters. Turn left after the red barn and follow the driveway up to the visitor center. Free maps indicating bicycle trails are available at the visitor center.

### Ride #1

This ride begins to the south or far end of the parking area at the trailhead for the Rift Zone Trail and the Bear Valley Trail. The Rift Zone branches off to the left and is illegal for mountain bikes. An easy .2-mile pedal will take you to the intersection with the Sky Trail, also illegal for mountain bikes, branching off to the right. Numerous hikers and other bikers will be encountered on this beautiful ride; please pedal slowly and always stay

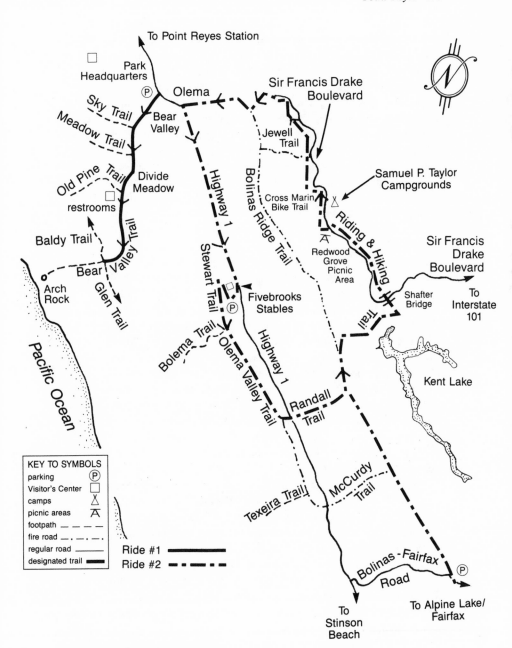

# POINT REYES
# RIDES #1 & #2

in control. Continue straight .6 mile past the intersection with Meadow Trail branching right and begin a gentle uphill climb .8 mile to Divide Meadow, Old Pine Trail (illegal for bikes) to the right, and rest rooms. Spend a few minutes here taking in the scenery and, perhaps if you are lucky like we were, enjoying a generous view of a bobcat gliding across the meadow. When you are ready, head straight and downhill through dense pines and a cool valley to the intersection of Bear, Glen, and Baldy trails. This is as far as you can ride; note the bike rack to the right for cyclists' convenience. The remaining trail crosses wilderness preserve and is illegal for bicycles. It is well worth locking your bike for the brief jaunt .8 mile down to Arch Rock and the beach. To return back to the parking area, head back the way you came.

### Ride #2

This ride may be started in a variety of locations: either Samuel P. Taylor State Park, Point Reyes Park Headquarters, or Fivebrooks Stables. This description will start at the parking area for Fivebrooks Stables just off Highway 1, beginning at the large dirt parking area and the Fivebrooks Trailhead. Ride .3 mile on the Stewart Trail to the intersection with the Rift Zone Trail and Olema Valley Trail. Bear left on the Olema Valley Trail. You will pass through several intersections closely packed and leading back to Fivebrooks Stables but continue on Olema Valley.

Grunt and groan 1.2 miles up to and past the intersection with Bolema Trail (illegal for bicycles) branching to the right; continue to the left on the Olema Trail. From here the trail rolls and descends predominantly on sandy and silty single track to the intersection with Randall Trail 1.3 miles away. Watch out for gopher holes that suddenly appear and bury your front wheel! Olema Valley Trail continues straight to Texeira Trail 2.3 miles away. Bear left, continuing on the Olema Valley Trail, and descend .4 mile to Highway 1. The start of Randall Trail begins immediately across Highway 1 and ascends for 1.7 miles to Bolinas Ridge Trail. The climb is terraced and steady; downshift and pace your climb and try practicing your mantras.

Once at Bolinas Ridge Trail, proceed through the gate and head left 1 mile to the intersection with Shafter Bridge Trail. The Shafter Bridge Trailhead is somewhat concealed and to the right, so stay alert; it will appear just after leaving the cover of trees and a short downhill. Should you encounter a cattle gate you have gone too far; turn around and look carefully for the trail now on your left. Shafter Bridge is a wild and whooping downhill rush 1.9 miles away. Stay in control; though the trail is mostly hard-pack, there are some loose spots that could make things a little more exciting than planned. At the bottom of the descent, a trail branches off

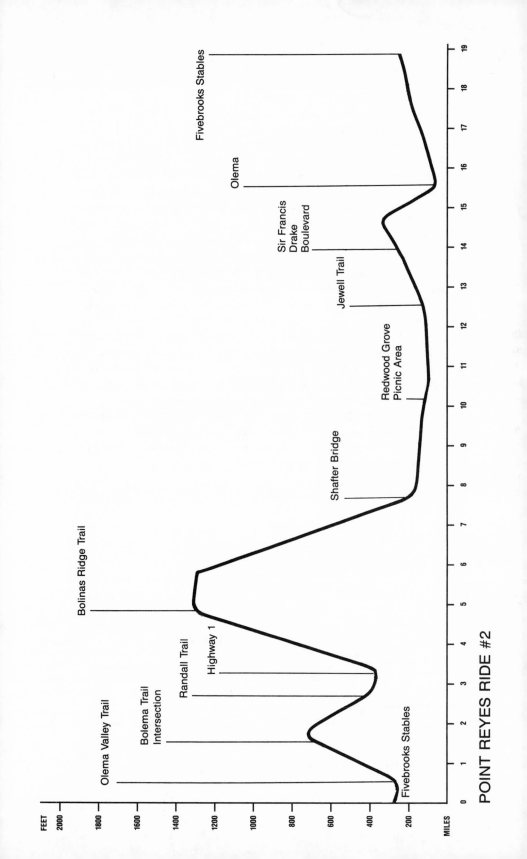

POINT REYES RIDE #2

to the right and toward the dam. Head straight, toward Shafter Bridge and Sir Francis Drake Boulevard.

Once at Shafter Bridge you have two options. We recommend picking your way on an unmarked trail under the bridge to the Riding and Hiking Trail on the other side of Papermill Creek. Bear left on the trail and ride 1.9 miles to the Irvine Picnic Area and a pedestrian bridge crossing Sir Francis Drake Boulevard. The route under Shafter Bridge may get your feet wet and is somewhat tricky; however, it avoids Sir Francis Drake Boulevard, which can be quite busy with cars and RVs. If you wish to avoid carrying your bike and crossing the creek, turn left on Sir Francis Drake Boulevard and ride approximately 1.9 miles to rejoin the Riding and Hiking Trail at Irvine Picnic Area and cross over the road on the pedestrian bridge. Pedal .5 mile to the Redwood Grove Picnic Area and Samuel P. Taylor State Park. Continue straight, past the campgrounds on a service road through the state park. The service road becomes a paved bicycle trail, which you will follow past the intersection with Jewell Trail at 2.2 miles. Proceed straight on the paved bicycle trail to Sir Francis Drake Boulevard 1.5 miles away and a left turn. The remaining 5.1-mile portion of this ride is on public highway — remember to use extreme caution. Pedal up and out of the canyon 1.8 miles on Sir Francis Drake Boulevard to the town of Olema and the intersection with Highway 1. At Olema, turn left and ride a rolling 3.3 miles on Highway 1 to the gravel turnoff for Fivebrooks Stables and the parking area.

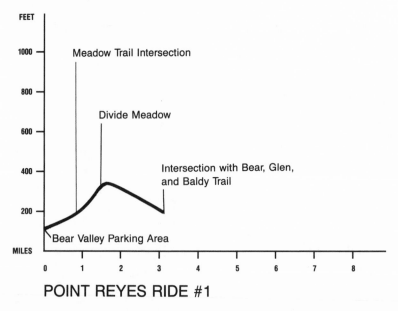

**POINT REYES RIDE #1**

## Chapter Twenty-Seven
# ANNADEL STATE PARK

*Ride #1*
**TRAILHEAD:** *North Burma Trail, Channel Drive*
**TOPO:** *Santa Rosa*
**OVERALL DIFFICULTY:** *Moderate*
**TECHNICAL DIFFICULTY:** *Moderate/Difficult*
**DISTANCE:** *8.6 miles*

*Ride #2*
**TRAILHEAD:** *Schultz Trail, Schultz Road*
**TOPO:** *Kenwood*
**OVERALL DIFFICULTY:** *Moderate*
**TECHNICAL DIFFICULTY:** *Moderate*
**DISTANCE:** *7.2 miles*

*Ride #3*
**TRAILHEAD:** *Schultz Trail, Schultz Road*
**TOPO:** *Kenwood and Santa Rosa*
**OVERALL DIFFICULTY:** *Moderate/Strenuous*
**TECHNICAL DIFFICULTY:** *Moderate*
**DISTANCE:** *13.5 miles*

*Highlights*

Nestled in Sonoma County, Annadel State Park's 5,000 acres of rolling, rocky terrain offer the visitor a stunning collage of intermittent streams, verdant meadows, and quiet woodlands.

The area was first frequented by the Southern Pomo and the Southern Wappo tribes. Though no permanent villages were established, the rocky

175

hills were important to the Native Americans as a source of obsidian, which they fashioned into scrapers, knives, arrowheads, and spear points. After 1770, the Spanish introduced farming and cattle ranching, which began replacing the Indian influence of hunting and gathering in the area.

In 1837, Annadel became part of a 19,000-acre Mexican land grant. Beginning in the 1880s, as San Francisco and other west coast cities were being built, the need for sheep- and cattle-grazing land in the vicinity was replaced by the demand for cobblestone material. A plentiful resource at Annadel, cobblestone quarrying became a major income source for several families. The daughter of one of the families even had the area named after her, "Annie's Dell," which later became the inspiration for the name of the park, Annadel.

When the demand for cobblestone faded in the 1920s, the land reverted back to agricultural use. Periodically, perlite, a derivative of obsidian used as insulation, was experimentally mined nearby. The area was purchased and designated a state park in 1971.

You will experience a wide range of environmental conditions within the park's boundaries: Douglas fir, chaparral, oaks, redwoods, and open meadows. This diversity affords the visitor a unique opportunity to view a tremendous variety of birds and other wildlife. The best months to view wild flowers are April and May, although many plants bloom beginning in January and continue until September.

*Rangers have reported an ever-expanding network of unauthorized trails and short cuts in areas that once had plants growing on them. Please help protect this beautiful and fragile area by remaining on authorized trails.*

### Getting There
Located near the city of Santa Rosa just east of Interstate 101. From San Francisco take 101 north to Highway 12 exit. Follow Highway 12 through Santa Rosa to Los Alamos Road. Turn right on Los Alamos to Montgomery Drive. Continue .5 mile to Channel Drive. Head left on Channel Drive to the park headquarters then 1 more mile to the main parking lot. From the East Bay follow Interstate 80 to Highway 29 toward Napa. Just after the junction of Highway 221 and 29 bear right on Highway 12/121. Remain on Highway 12 through Sonoma and Kenwood. Shortly after passing through Kenwood you will turn left on Los Alamos Road, right on Montgomery Drive and then left on Channel Drive.

### Ride #1
Beginning at the small parking area in front of the park headquarters, bear right on Channel Drive, pedal .3 mile, and turn right on North Burma Trail. The trail climbs quickly through a boulder-strewn path; it may be

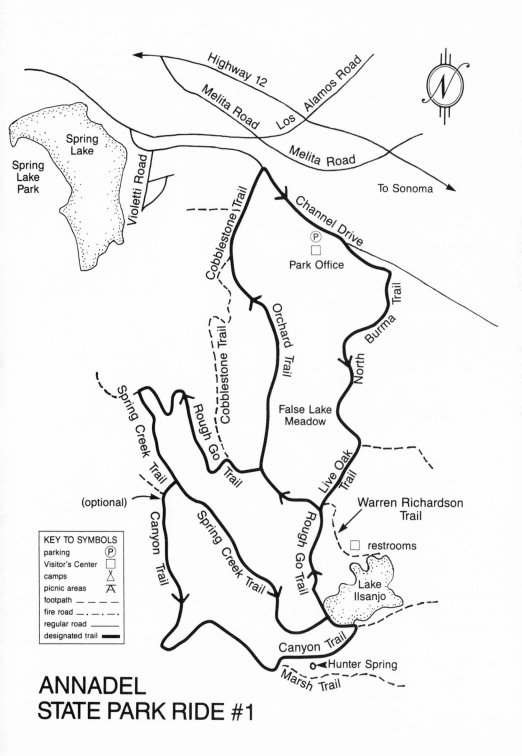

# ANNADEL
# STATE PARK RIDE #1

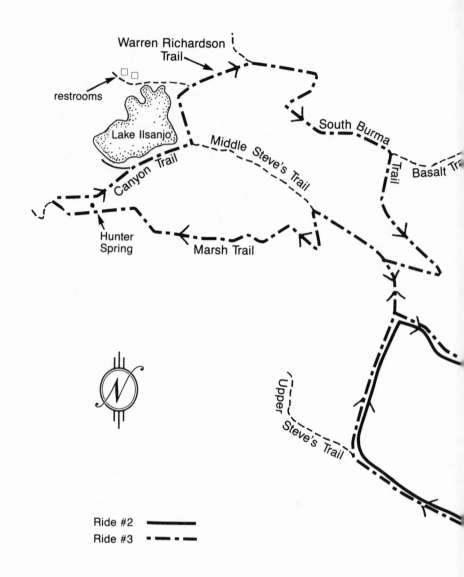

Ride #2 ───────
Ride #3 ·─·─·─

# ANNADEL STATE PARK
# RIDE #2 & #3

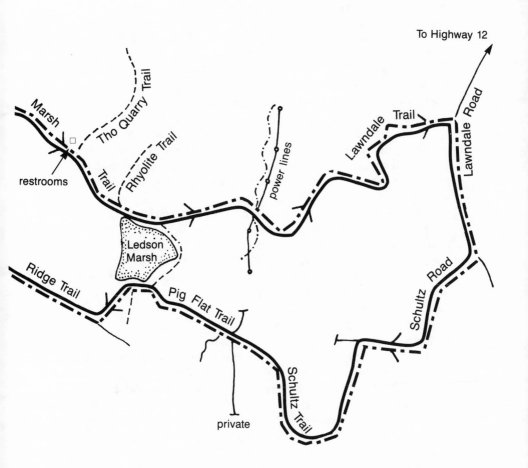

KEY TO SYMBOLS
parking ⓟ
Visitor's Center ☐
camps △
picnic areas ⚊A⚊
footpath ⎯ ⎯ ⎯ ⎯
fire road ⎯ . ⎯ . ⎯ .
regular road ⎯⎯⎯⎯
designated trail ▬▬▬

To Highway 12

Lawndale Road

Lawndale Trail

Schultz Road

power lines

Marsh
Tho Quarry Trail
Rhyolite Trail
Trail
restrooms

Ledson Marsh

Ridge Trail

Pig Flat Trail

Schultz Trail

private

necessary to dismount and walk your bike over some large rocks. After 1.5 miles of this technical challenge and uphill effort is the intersection with Live Oak Trail. Bear right on Live Oak and ride .4 mile across open and level meadow to the intersection with Rough Go Trail and Warren Richardson Trail. Turn right on Rough Go and begin to gain firsthand knowledge of why this trail was named "Rough Go." The next 1.5 miles may turn your knuckles white, jar your kidneys, and stretch your level of sanity. Take this very, very rocky descent slowly and look for a path between the rocks. After .3 mile you will pass the intersection with Orchard Trail to the right. Remember this cutoff, as you will later follow it for the return trip to your car. Continue straight on Rough Go, passing Cobblestone after .2 mile, to Spring Creek Trail 1 mile later.

Head left on Spring Creek (at wooden bridge) for .5 mile of level cycling to the intersection with Canyon Trail heading right. Here you have an option. You can continue left on Spring Creek, climbing gently 1.3 miles to the intersection with Rough Go Trail at the dam and overlooking Lake Ilsanjo. Or bear right on Canyon Trail, climb steadily past the intersection with Marsh Trail and picnic area at 1.6 miles, descend .6 mile, passing Hunter Spring to Lake Ilsanjo. Here you will bear left, skirting Lake Ilsanjo, and pedal .2 mile across the dam to the Spring Creek Trail intersection.

Either way, once at the dam, head straight on Rough Go .5 mile to the intersection with Warren Richardson and Live Oak trails. Rough Go lives up to its name again as you bear left on the .3-mile section you had previously ridden. Bear right at Orchard Trail and across the meadow. The trail climbs and dips, sometimes suddenly (Michael was reintroduced to his bike's top tube during one sudden, root-filled transition), the next 1.1 miles until meeting Cobblestone Trail.

At Cobblestone descend .8 mile. (There is one confusing section to beware of. You will encounter an unmarked trail branching to the left and across an open meadow toward the west and Spring Lake Park. Stay right and continue descending toward the housing developments below.) At the housing developments, you will rejoin Channel Drive. Bear right and pedal .4 mile back to the park headquarters.

### Rides #2 & #3
### Getting There
Located near the city of Santa Rosa just east of Interstate 101. From San Francisco take 101 north to Highway 12 exit. Follow Highway 12 through Santa Rosa to Lawndale Road. Turn right on Lawndale and drive to the parking area on the right and the trailhead for Lawndale Trail. From the East Bay follow Interstate 80 to Highway 29 toward Napa. Just after the Highway 221 and 29 junction bear right on Highway 12/121. Remain on

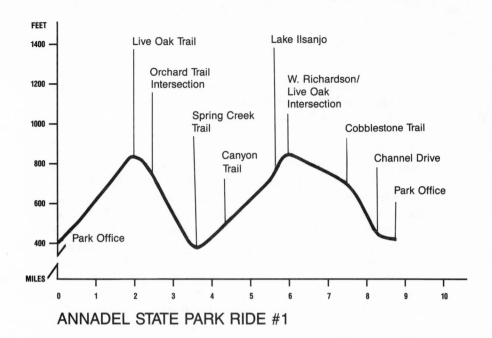

**ANNADEL STATE PARK RIDE #1**

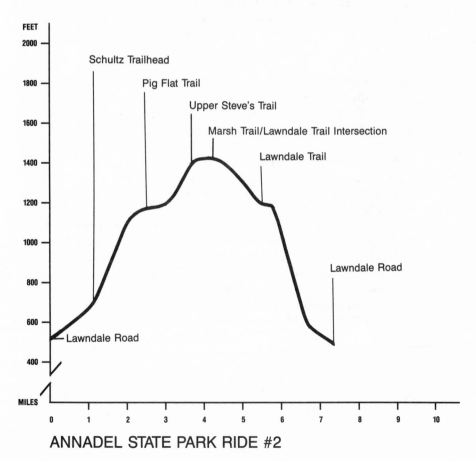

**ANNADEL STATE PARK RIDE #2**

Highway 12 through Sonoma and Kenwood. Shortly after passing through Kenwood, turn left on Lawndale Road and drive to the parking area on the right and the trailhead for Lawndale Trail.

### Ride #2

Beginning at the parking lot, pedal up Lawndale Road to a right turn on Schultz Road. At approximately 1.3 miles and just before the road hooks to the left, a dirt road with a gate will be encountered; pass through this gate and begin riding on Schultz Trail. Climb steadily 1.65 miles through scrub brush to the intersection with Pig Flat Trail; head straight .5 mile through mostly open meadow and the intersection with Marsh Trail. Bear left .4 mile to the intersection with Ridge Trail. Turn right and parallel the fence line .7 mile on flat, open terrain passing Upper Steve's Trail; bear right and pedal .7 mile to Marsh Trail (Ride #3 description starts here). Ride #2, however, bears right on Marsh Trail for 1.2 miles, passing Two Quarry and Rhyolite trails, both branching to the left. Bear left at the intersection with Lawndale Trail; after approximately .3 mile you will travel under a power line and begin a rapid 1.5-mile descent (beware of hikers) to Lawndale Road and the parking lot.

### Ride #3

Follow the description for Ride #2 to the intersection with Marsh and Ridge trails. Bear left on Marsh Trail .8 mile, passing South Burma Trail and Middle Steve's Trail, to the Canyon Trail intersection. (The next 1.6 miles of Marsh Trail are quite rough and all downhill; make certain your dentures are well glued.) At the intersection with Canyon Trail, bear right and continue down .6 mile past Hunter Spring to Lake Ilsanjo. Keep right, skirting Lake Ilsanjo .3 mile to the intersection with Middle Steve's Trail. Head left .3 mile to the intersection with Warren Richardson Trail and make a right turn.

Climb steadily .4 mile and head right on South Burma Trail; climb steadily 1.1 miles past the Basalt Trail. Shortly after this intersection, South Burma levels and then drops to the junction with Marsh Trail, .9 mile later. Bear left on Marsh Trail 1.5 miles passing intersections with Ridge, Two Quarry, and Rhyolite trails to the junction with Lawndale Trail. Ride a level .3 mile, passing under a power line, and begin a 1.5-mile descent (beware of hikers) to Lawndale Road and the parking lot.

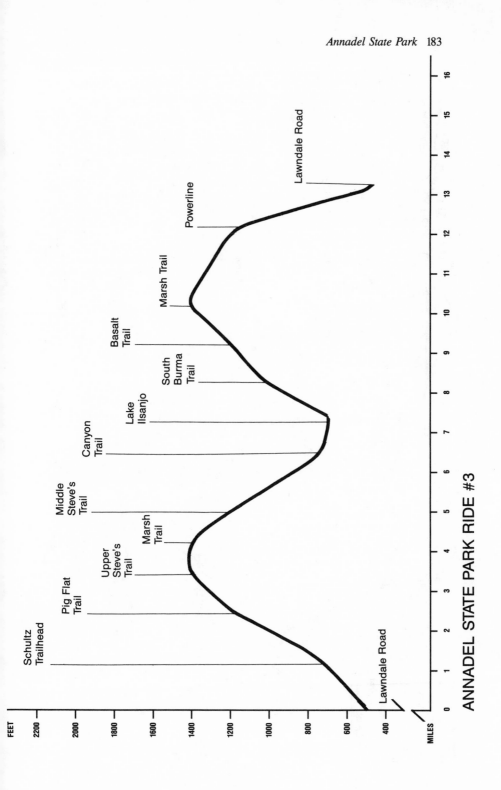

ANNADEL STATE PARK RIDE #3

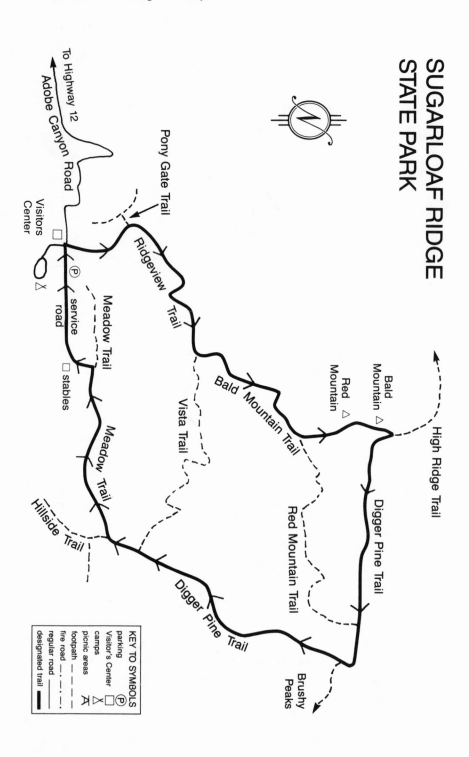

SUGARLOAF RIDGE
STATE PARK

To Highway 12
Adobe Canyon Road

Pony Gate Trail

Visitors
Center

Ridgeview Trail

service road

Meadow Trail

stables

Meadow Trail

Vista Trail

Bald Mountain Trail

Red Mountain

Bald Mountain

Red Mountain

High Ridge Trail

Digger Pine Trail

Red Mountain Trail

Hillside Trail

Digger Pine Trail

Brushy Peaks

KEY TO SYMBOLS
parking                        Ⓟ
Visitor's Center               □
camps                          △
picnic areas                   ▲
footpath            – . . –
fire road           – . – . –.
regular road        _____
designated trail    ▬▬▬▬▬

## Chapter Twenty-Eight
# SUGARLOAF STATE PARK

**TRAILHEAD:** *Ridge View*
**TOPO:** *Rutherford and Kenwood*
**OVERALL DIFFICULTY:** *Strenuous*
**TECHNICAL DIFFICULTY:** *Moderate*
**DISTANCE:** *6.3 miles*

### Highlights
Sugarloaf State Park extends over 2,500 acres and ranges in elevation from 600 feet at the park entrance to 2,729 feet atop Bald Mountain. Near Annadel State Park and tucked into the wilds of Sonoma County, Sugarloaf is an area widely diverse in plant and wildlife. Whether exploring the high chaparral ridges of Bald Mountain or wandering through the dense groves of trees and sprawling meadows of the Sonoma Creek Drainage, the visitor will find much to enjoy. Some of California's largest big-leaf maple trees can be found here (a good reason to visit in the fall to enjoy the spectacular colors and cooler temperatures) along with madrone, coast redwood, and several varieties of oak.

In springtime the area explodes with color from California poppies, cream cups, lupine, penstemon, thistles, buttercups, Indian pinks, brodiaea, and many others. If you travel early, quietly, and with your senses alert, you may have the pleasure of viewing some of the abundant wildlife that this park offers. Blacktail deer, raccoons, bobcats, gray fox, rabbits, squirrels, and weasels all make their home here.

Although the ascent of Bald Mountain is quite strenuous (more than 2,100 feet in less than 3 miles), those with the strength and desire will be rewarded with grandeur and a great feeling of accomplishment!

### Getting There

Located near the city of Santa Rosa just east of Interstate 101. From San Francisco take 101 north to Highway 12 exit. Follow Highway 12 through Santa Rosa to Adobe Canyon Road. Turn left on Adobe Canyon Road and drive to the park entrance and the parking area for all trails. From the East Bay you will follow Interstate 80 to Highway 29 toward Napa. Just after the Highway 221 and 29 junction bear right on Highway 12/121. Remain on Highway 12 through Sonoma and Kenwood. Shortly after passing through Kenwood you will turn right on Adobe Canyon Road and drive to the park entrance and the parking area for all trails.

### The Ride

Beginning at the visitor's center, pedal up the Stern Trail .5 mile to an intersection with Pony Gate Trail on the left, a dirt road with a no trespassing sign heading straight, and a gate marking the beginning of pavement to the right. Our path is to the right and begins climbing steeply at this point; you will remain on the pavement, rough at times, for 1.8 miles, passing several intersections branching off to the right. At 1.8 miles the pavement continues to the left and a cluster of microwave towers. Although temptation will pull you in this direction, our path will lead us right and up the somewhat ridiculously steep-looking rocky-climb-from-hell.

Although the summit has no redeeming features, the view from the top makes the .4-mile ride/walk/crawl worthwhile! We recommend a lunch stop on Bald Mountain's 2,729-foot peak. High Ridge Trail branches to the left while you descend via the Digger Pine Trail to the right; you will encounter several brief uphills, although they are easy compared with what you have already endured. The next 2.5 miles to a stream crossing and the intersection with Meadow Trail are quite loose, rocky, and rutted with several washouts due to heavy equestrian usage and erosion. (*NOTE: Sugarloaf is one of the most popular areas for equestrians to train for endurance events. Mountain bikers are reminded to remain in control and yield the right-of-way at all times.*)

Just past the stream crossing, bear right on Meadow Trail .8 mile to the Group Camp and stables. At this point leave the trail and bear left heading past the stables on the service road .3 mile back to the parking lot.

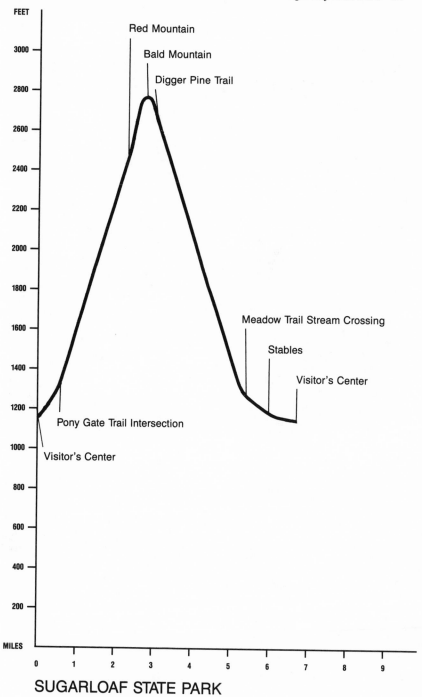

FEET

3000

2800

2600

2400

2200

2000

1800

1600

1400

1200

1000

800

600

400

200

MILES

Red Mountain

Bald Mountain

Digger Pine Trail

Meadow Trail Stream Crossing

Stables

Visitor's Center

Pony Gate Trail Intersection

Visitor's Center

0    1    2    3    4    5    6    7    8    9

SUGARLOAF STATE PARK

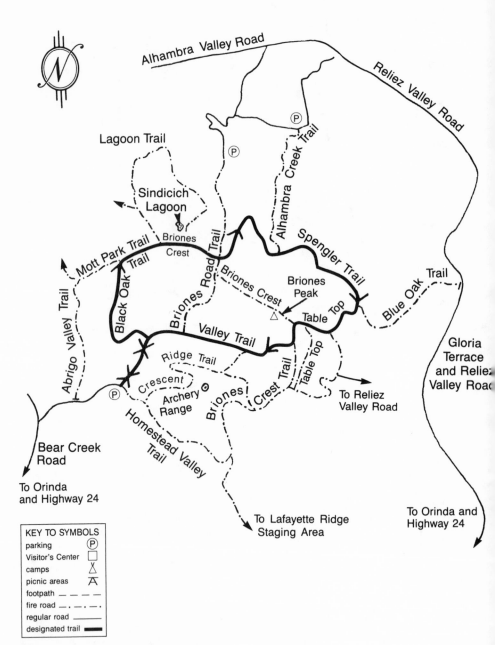

# BRIONES REGIONAL PARK

## Chapter Twenty-Nine
# BRIONES REGIONAL PARK

**TRAILHEAD:** *Old Briones Road/Bear Creek*
**TOPO:** *Briones Valley, Walnut Creek*
**OVERALL DIFFICULTY:** *Moderate/Strenuous*
**TECHNICAL DIFFICULTY:** *Moderate*
**DISTANCE:** *Approximately 8.7 miles*

### Highlights
Briones Regional Park is a delightfully undeveloped 5,484 acres of rolling grassland, oak woodland, verdant canyons, and hidden meadows. Since the early 1800s much of Briones' history has revolved around cattle ranching. For a short time, during the 1850s and '60s, the Alhambra Valley became an important fruit-growing area with large orchards and vineyards; the gnarled remains of many of these orchards are still evident today.

In 1957, Contra Costa County and the East Bay Regional Park District established Briones as a large open space park in the Bear Creek Watershed. With additional annexing of land, the East Bay Regional Park District created a park full of scenic trails perfect for hiking, biking, and equestrian use. This is truly a magical park to explore and enjoy.

### Getting There
Located just northwest of Walnut Creek and north of the Caldecott Tunnel on Highway 24. From Highway 24 and the town of Orinda head north on Camino Pablo Road. Drive to Bear Creek Road, where you will turn right, following Bear Creek past Briones Dam to the park entrance.

### The Ride
Beginning at the Bear Creek entrance and parking area for Old Briones

Road Trailhead, pedal .7 mile through a gate and up a slight grade to the intersection with Black Oak Trail. Bear left on the Black Oak Trail and a steep climb — we walked — of several hundred yards to the top of the ridge. The next 1.1 miles are mostly rolling, following the ridge with several sharp ups and downs. At the Mott Peak Trail, turn right and descend to the Briones Crest Trail, .4 mile away. Head right on the Briones Crest Trail, skirting Sindicich Lagoon (more of a cattle wallow) to Old Briones Road. Turn left on Old Briones Road, then right on Spengler Trail, .5 mile away. (The remaining miles back to the parking area will take you through numerous cattle gates. Please be sure to leave them as you found them — closed or open. Also, in wet weather the track can get very muddy — have fun, but use caution.)

The Spengler Trail descends 1.2 miles to the intersection with Alhambra Creek Trail. The valley is often very lush and wet but always beautiful. Continue on Spengler Trail and climb over one small ridge, into another very green canyon, and onto another ridge, meeting up with Blue Oak Trail at .7 mile. Enjoy a well-deserved rest and take in the view before continuing on. Spengler Trail drops and climbs quickly before intersecting with Table Top Trail bearing right, 1 mile later. At Table Top, head left and begin a sharp and arduous .5-mile ascent to the top and Briones Crest Trail.

Before turning left and descending on the Briones Crest Trail, make the short climb up to Briones Peak (1,483 feet) — if you have the stamina and energy, the view is well worth it. At .5 mile head right and continue descending to the Valley Trail. (If you wish to lengthen your journey with a very picturesque addition, continue straight on Briones Crest, up a short rise, past the Crescent Ridge Trail, and down to the Homestead Valley Trail. Turn right on Homestead Valley and follow it back to Old Briones Road and a left turn to the parking area.) Our path takes us 1 very choppy mile — cattle and horses erode the track when wet — to Old Briones Road. Turn left on Old Briones Road and pedal 1.1 miles back to the parking area.

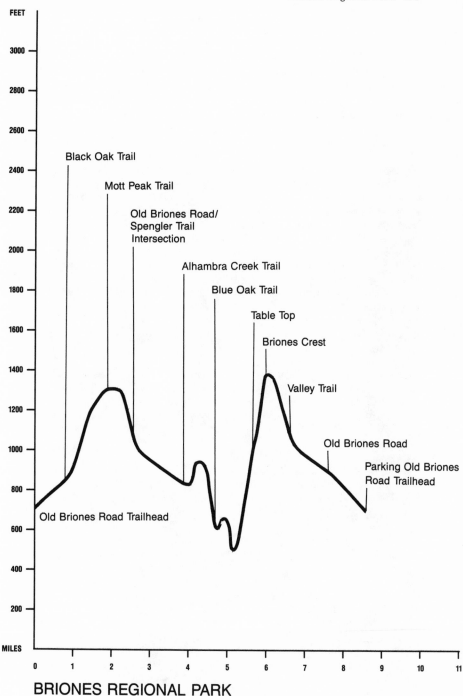

FEET

3000

2800

2600

2400 — Black Oak Trail

2200 — Mott Peak Trail

Old Briones Road/
Spengler Trail
Intersection

2000

Alhambra Creek Trail

1800

Blue Oak Trail

1600

Table Top

Briones Crest

1400

Valley Trail

1200

Old Briones Road

1000

Parking Old Briones
Road Trailhead

800

Old Briones Road Trailhead

600

400

200

MILES

0    1    2    3    4    5    6    7    8    9    10    11

# BRIONES REGIONAL PARK

# More Legal Rides Around the Bay Area

Not every trail or area is described in detail within the pages of this guide. That would take too much space (imagine lugging a 10-pound volume around with you) and would also preclude the wonderful joy of self-discovery. What follows is a concise listing of other parks and preserves around the Bay Area that, at the time we went to press, offered legal mountain bike rides longer than one or two miles. Happy Trails!

### Midpeninsula Regional Open Space District
WINDY HILL OPEN SPACE: Grassy ridges and woodland ravines characterize the special attraction of this preserve, which is located just off Skyline Boulevard, east of Highway 84 and overlooking Palo Alto. Spring Ridge Trail, 3 miles each way, is the only trail legal for bikes.

PURISIMA CREEK REDWOODS: Located on the western slopes of the Santa Cruz Mountains and overlooking Half Moon Bay, the preserve is known for its towering redwoods and lush undergrowth of ferns, berries and wild flowers. Whittemore Gulch, Harkins Fire Trail and Purisima Creek Road are legal for bikes and offer approximately 6 miles of pedaling opportunity.

### East Bay Regional Park District
SUNOL REGIONAL PARK: Located just off Interstate 680, northeast of Fremont, Sunol is probably best known for the scenic gorge on Alameda Creek. Little Yosemite, as the gorge is called, is a wonderful respite from a hot pedal during the late spring or early summer. Camp Ohlone Road, Cerro Este Road, Cave Rocks Road, and Hayfield Road offer nearly 7 miles of cycling opportunity.

LAFAYETTE-MORAGA REGIONAL TRAIL: This trail is a 7.6-mile linear park designed for equestrian, hiking and biking use and parallels St. Mary's Road through Lafayette and Moraga.

193

### East Bay Municipal Water District

LAFAYETTE RESERVOIR: Located just off Mt. Diablo Boulevard near Walnut Creek, it offers families an excellent place to pedal using the Shore Trail, a 2.8-mile winding and paved trail that completely encircles the reservoir.

SAN PABLO RESERVOIR: Tucked in among Wildcat, Tilden, and Briones Regional Parks, the area provides 4.3 miles of level trail running the length of the reservoir.

### State Parks

CHINA CAMP STATE PARK: Just north of San Rafael via US 101, biking is legal on Ridge Road, Back Ranch Meadows Trail, Miwok Trail, and Jake's Island Trail, offering approximately 5 miles of pedaling.

JACK LONDON STATE PARK: Located near the town of Glen Ellen, south of the Sonoma Highway and Annadel State Park, Jack London State Park offers approximately 3 miles of pedaling on the Mountain Trail, Lower Treadmill Road, and Hayfields Trail.

# Appendix

**Mountain Bikes Are Not the Environmental Disaster Some Claim, But...**

*The following is an amended version of an article by Michael Hodgson that ran in the* San Jose Mercury News.

Since its inception, mountain biking has lived a double life, flirting with both popularity and condemnation. On the one hand, it is loved and enjoyed by millions as a legitimate form of outdoor recreation, bike hiking if you will. On the other hand, mountain biking is maligned as a primary cause of increased trail erosion and trail use conflicts, an unwelcome addition to parkland trails.

It is quite clear, however, that love them or hate them, mountain bikes are here to stay and are continuing to increase in popularity. What of the accusations of environmental impact and user conflicts with the oft-mentioned, but seldom caught minority of renegades on wheels reaping havoc on the trails?

As far as environmental impact, several studies conducted by private individuals and government agencies indicate that mountain bikes have no more impact on the trails than do hikers.

According to Joe Seney's research report, presented to the Association of American Geographers in 1990 and conducted through the Department of Earth Science, Montana State University, as part of his master's thesis, "It is difficult to distinguish bicycle impact from hiker impact on the measures of water runoff, sediment runoff, or soil compaction."

Seney's report further elaborates that equestrian use produced significantly more sediment runoff than either biking or hiking use. Sediment runoff is directly related to erosional loss of soil. Equestrian use was also linked to significantly less water runoff than use by either hikers or bicyclists. Water runoff is necessary to prevent swampy trail conditions.

The discovery that equestrian use has more impact on a given trail than mountain bike use leaves mountain bikers understandably miffed when

195

land managers close a trail to them, citing environmental damage, yet continue to leave the trail open to horses.

If mountain bikes are not a significant environmental threat as Seney indicates, what of the widespread accusations of rutted and chewed-up terrain caused by mountain bikes?

One can look at two factors in the quest for an answer: trail construction and user responsibility. Seney's study found that trail construction, not trail use, was the primary culprit behind user impacts. Well-designed and well-constructed trails stood up to all types of use. Steep trails suffered the most damage by all users. Trails with a slope angle of more than 15 percent led to associated erosional problems.

Of course, even on a well-constructed trail, irresponsible use can lead to irreversible trail impacts. When was the last time you saw a hiker executing a power slide around a turn? According to land managers, mountain bikers must ride under control at all times, no skidding or sliding. Further, both equestrians and mountain bikers must stay off muddy trails, and all trail users must stay on designated trails and not cut switchbacks.

The number-one reason for trail closure to mountain bikes, though, is user conflict. When mountain bikers are an actual or perceived threat to other trail users, the trail usually gets closed to bike use.

"Safety is a primary issue for us," says Mary Hale, public communications coordinator for Midpeninsula Open Space District. "While it's true that only about 3 percent of all mountain bikers are inconsiderate and negligent, one or two serious incidents involving mountain bikers and (hikers or equestrians) create a liability concern and perceived danger that must be accounted for."

Unfortunately, most public lands are understaffed and underfunded, leaving most trail users to fend for themselves and creating situations where rules that are made are often unenforceable.

As a result, land managers, unable to effectively patrol trails against the "small groups of renegade users," tend to use possible trail closures as a kind of "sword of Damocles," hoping the majority will find a way to police their own.

Peter Fournier, former president of ROMP (Responsible Organized Mountain Pedalers), participates in a volunteer bike patrol, Bikewatch, for Santa Clara County Parks and Recreation, but he states emphatically that the bike patrol's only purpose is one of education, not policing. Education instead of confrontation is the key to acceptance, according to Don Douglass, former president of the International Mountain Biking Association. That approach has realized results.

In 1990, following a series of national meetings with mountain biking organizations and land-use managers, the Wilderness Society, previously anti-mountain bike, reversed its stance and endorsed "appropriate and expanded use for mountain bikes on public lands (other than wilderness)."

Also throwing its weight behind mountain bike use on nonwilderness trails in 1990 was the American Hiking Society. The AHS stated, ". . . public trails should be available to all compatible uses, and mountain bicycles generally are compatible when operated responsibly."

Through education, the old argument that horses and mountain bikes cannot coexist on the same trails has generally been laid to rest. Local events, "Ride for the Ridge Trail"' sponsored by the Bicycle Trails Council of the East Bay, and "ROMP and STOMP," cosponsored by ROMP and the Los Altos Hills Horseman's Association, have been instrumental in demonstrating that horses and bikes can utilize the same trails—providing bikers and equestrians ride responsibly.

Assuming that everyone eventually agrees mountain biking is a legitimate form of recreation in public parks, lands and forests, should mountain bikes be given access to all backcountry areas, including wilderness?

In an unscientific survey of current mountain bikers, conducted for this article, the majority said no. There are places that mountain bikes don't belong. Trails where proven and potential trail use conflicts are unresolvable and hazardous to all users, areas where environmental impacts are proven, and all wilderness areas.

Michael McCoy, author and avid mountain biker had this to say in a 1990 *Trilogy Magazine* article, "Mountain bikes are an efficient and fun means of getting out into nature and exploring the outdoors. But the wilderness doesn't need mountain bikes, and mountain bikers don't need the wilderness."

"Wilderness is for leaving behind our high-tech gadgetry and slowing down our need-for-speed temperaments," he adds. "Moreover, wilderness areas exist for the protection of ecosystems—do not disturb zones for the plants and animals that have no say in what man does to the rest of the planet."

### Some Mountain Bikers Have the Wrong Attitude

*The following is an amended version of an article by Michael Hodgson that appeared in the* San Jose Mercury News.

Hiking with a friend through Long Ridge Open Space not so long ago, I came face to face with the ugly side of mountain biking—a side that certainly gives land managers pause when considering access issues.

On a wet and muddy single track, one that shouldn't have been ridden on even if it had been open (which it wasn't), I encountered no less than seven mountain bikers. They weren't in one group (two groups of two and one of three) and they weren't wild and woolly renegades out to blast mud and rip turf. Instead, they were all well dressed, riding expensive bikes and old enough to know better — if there is an such age when moral fortitude becomes the norm.

What was most distressing about the encounters was not the fact that all were riding illegally on a trail marked closed because of wet and easily damaged terrain, although I admit to a mild facial twitch and a desire to throttle the next biker that happened by and scream "What the hell are you thinking!" It wasn't even the fact that the trail was becoming rutted and thrashed from previous biker forays along this closed trail.

I am riled up because these thoughtless bikers and the obvious trail damage caused by other free-wheeling renegades have removed any chance I once had of convincing my friend, and now all whom my friend comes in contact with, that mountain bikers are responsible trail users and should be allowed equal access to the great outdoors. All the columns, articles and books that I have written defending mountain bikers and their right to area trails come pouring back down on me and the weight is unforgiving.

It becomes so easy to point fingers at the other guy, the other thoughtless soul who rides irresponsibly, but the glaring truth is these other guys are still part of the collective we, the mountain biking community. To be fair, the equestrian fraternity has its thoughtless riders too as evidenced by several hoof prints chewing down the middle of the same trail, also closed to horses.

Still, the flames of contention burn hottest on the subject of mountain biking. And, unfortunately, it is the thoughtless acts of those admittedly few riders that fuel the fires singing individuals and organizations who are working so hard to project a positive image of mountain biking.

In any area where multiple use is allowed, even encouraged, each individual use becomes a privilege, not a right. Hiking, horseback riding, mountain biking, and trail running are all legitimate uses of our area trails, but when one or more of those uses begins to infringe upon the safety and enjoyment of the trails by other groups or even damage the land itself, then its use must be questioned. So it is with mountain biking.

Peter Fournier, former president of Responsible Organized Mountain Pedalers (ROMP), views irresponsible bikers with similar contempt but quickly adds that banning mountain bikes from the trails is not an answer.

"We have drunk drivers and careless motorists all over our highways, and yet we don't talk of closing the roads. Instead, we step up enforcement of rules. What we have to face is the fact that we need to have enforcement in our parks in a similar manner as our freeways," states Fournier.

"Trails throughout the Bay used to be quiet sanctuaries where we didn't need a lot of rules or require extensive enforcement of those rules because visitation was light. All that has changed with the dramatic increase in use," adds Fournier. "We have to convince local land managers that they need to get out there and step up enforcement and if they don't we will continue to see law breakers."

Area land managers from both Midpeninsula Open Space District and the East Bay Regional Park District agree that increased enforcement would be nice, but don't understand how anyone can expect them to accomplish that on a limited budget—no matter how you slice the pie, increased enforcement isn't financially feasible.

The one possibility that has been alluded to in conversations with Mid Pen is complete closure of an area to mountain bikes since focused enforcement at trailheads becomes easier than scattered enforcement over an entire trail network. Not a pleasant alternative for either party, but if mountain bikers cannot take it upon themselves to respect the rules and ride responsibly (and that admonition goes for any trail user) then they just might suffer the ignominy of having nowhere to ride.

### Future Trail Access for Cyclists Rests on Your Shoulders
*Get Involved in Your Community—Join a Bike Club*
By Peter Fournier, former President of ROMP (Responsible Organized Mountain Pedalers)

There may come a day when mountain cyclists are accepted by the entire trail-using community as equals, with a vested right to share the same trails, but it hasn't happened yet.

Often it takes only a small number of incidents and complaints on the part of trail users to give land managers justification to close trails to cyclists. Cyclists have the reputation of causing conflict, whether actual accidents or perceived conflict. To a great extent, access will be for those who cause the least amount of trouble (read additional expenditure for patrols and lawsuits) for park and open space managers.

Our parks and open space are suffering massive budget cuts in recent years. Many programs suffer as a result, with labor and time intensive activities such as park patrols a likely target. In the absence of adequate enforcement of the rules on our trails, it is not enough to claim that "a few" thoughtless individuals cause the problem. It is enough that a problem exists, real or perceived.

Now for the good news. There is much that you can do, as an individual, to protect your access to trails. I divide these actions into four categories: personal behavior, public relations, environmental care and group involvement.

Your personal behavior is, in one sense, all that matters to trail access. If your presence on the trail causes physical damage, whether to the trail or other trail users, injury, fear and trepidation, or merely unease, you are having a negative impact. This is where etiquette comes in. The International Mountain Biking Association (IMBA), publishes rules of the trail which are a good starting point to correct behavior when using public trails. Beyond these rules, a little common sense and empathy are indicated.

It isn't enough to simply obey the letter of the posted rules. Think about how your actions might be perceived. Riding quickly past a hiker, even on a wide road, may be perceived as threatening, or just plain annoying. On a single-track trail, if a hiker moves off the trail for you and you pass by, their perception may be that they were "run off the trail." Make no mistake, they will freely share their experience with other trail users, friends, family, colleagues, and park managers. It isn't a question of who is right, or even what the truth is. Perception becomes fact to many people.

Often cyclists forget their responsibility to other cyclists. I have been annoyed on many occasions by the lack of courtesy of another cyclist. Slow down to pass approaching cyclists, keep the dust down, warn when passing, and yield to uphill cyclists on narrow trails.

It's important to be safe, since any accident of which a ranger is aware of will be reported, and becomes a statistical black mark against cyclists. An injury accident is even worse, and an accident involving another trail user is the worst. Even if a helmet is not required in your park, wear one. Head injuries can be fatal at five miles per hour.

Public relations means simply how you relate to the public (that's them), and how they relate to you. I believe the best way to improve our image is to get involved in public service. Volunteering to build or maintain trails is an excellent way to show that you care about the trails you use, and that you're willing to put your own time and labor to use. Mountain biking is relatively new to our trails, and many people feel we have not earned our riding privilege by giving back to the parks. If you volunteer, you will meet these people, and your actions will begin to change their minds.

Don't leave out other forms of volunteerism. Volunteer work which does not directly benefit cycling is important. Consider docent work, educational programs, or anything else your park or open space agency offers.

Potential bicycle impact on a trail's surface and surrounding land is a major issue. Be aware that the continuous track left by a tire is simply more abhorrent to many than a boot or hoof print. Avoid riding in mud (I know it's fun, but it leaves a deep groove for water to follow, causing erosion). Skidding around corners is counterproductive to fast cornering, annoying to others, and damaging to the trail surface. Banking corners causes soil loss and erosion and is unsightly to others. Cutting new trails is probably the most obvious destructive activity. Why ruin the view for everyone?

Your involvement in a local cycling organization is really just a way to increase the effectiveness of your personal actions, by reaching and working with other cyclists, and providing a positive image to agencies and the public. Your support of these organizations will help to open and keep trails for cyclists.

The responsibility for future trail access for cyclists rests with you. Follow the posted rules of the trail, as well as the IMBA Rules of the Trail, help build and maintain your local trails, keep abreast of current issues, support local trail access events, go to public agency meetings and hearings, talk to other cyclists about safety and etiquette, and join your local club, as well as IMBA. Most of all, get involved. You don't have to do everything, but you can do something.

# Cycling Necessities

TIRE IRONS
PATCH KIT
SPARE TUBE
TIRE PUMP
CHAIN TOOL
APPROPRIATE SELECTION OF TIRE WRENCHES: check with bike
   shop
SPOKE WRENCH
SPARE SPOKES: (for your wheel type) these can be taped to the chain stay
CHANGE FOR A PHONE CALL
FIRST AID KIT: assorted bandages, ace bandage, 3x3 gauze pads,
   adhesive tape, moleskin, aspirin, antiseptic, tincture of Benzoin, needle,
   matches, sunscreen, water purification tablets. (Adventure Medical Kits
   in Berkeley and Atwater and Carey in Boulder, Colorado, manufacture
   special first aid kits for mountain bikers.)
WATER BOTTLE: Your body needs a minimum of two quarts of fluid
   per day, so plan accordingly!
COMPASS
SMALL LIGHT: flashlight, headlamp, or bike light
HIGH-ENERGY MUNCHIES: gorp, nuts, cheese, dried fruit

For an overnight add the following items to the above list:
MOUNTAIN BIKE REAR PANNIER RACK: Even if you are opting not
   to use panniers, the rack gives you a surface to which you can attach
   a tent and sleeping bag and also minimizes the inevitable brown racing
   stripe on your back in wet and muddy terrain.
SMALL BIKE PANNIERS AND/OR LARGE FANNY PACK: use
   whatever system maintains optimum agility and balance
SMALL STOVE AND FUEL
COMPACT COOK POT, 1 TO 2 QUARTS

COMPACT AND LIGHTWEIGHT DOWN SLEEPING BAG
COMPACT AND LIGHTWEIGHT TENT/BIVI SACK
SMALL KNIFE
SMALL SPOON
WATERPROOF/WINDPROOF MATCHES

# The Well-Dressed Rider

With the exception of shorts and helmet, riding attire can be adequately improvised with clothing that you may already own. Following is a list that will span the broad range of temperatures that can occur in the Bay Area. As with all active sports, layers must be thin and lightweight to allow for exact temperature adjustments; no single layer should be exceptionally warm. With the exception of t-shirts and socks, it is best to avoid cotton, which dries slowly and ends up feeling as if you are wearing a wet dishrag after only several hours of pedaling.

HELMET: An absolute necessity. Spend as much as you can possibly afford (how much is your head worth?); this is not a place to try and save some money! We recommend a helmet with some sort of shell on the exterior; this will help protect your head from sharp objects and extend the helmet's life.

SHORTS: Specialized cycling shorts are well worth the money. After spending several hours in the saddle those seemingly innocent seams on the butt of your walking shorts can feel like mountain ridges. We recommend Lycra or wool with a chamois or synthetic crotch pad.

SHOES: These should be stiff soled and provide good traction when walking becomes a necessity. Specific mountain biking boots are nice, but hiking footwear, low- or high-top, can be substituted with good results; check to be sure they operate with toe clips.

GLOVES: Make sure they have dense padding in the palms. Lightweight cross-country ski gloves work great for early mornings or cold days.

SHIRT: Cycling jerseys with back pockets are nice, but a cotton t-shirt works just fine. Avoid Lycra — it's clammy!

SUNGLASSES: These do much more than go along for the ride to make you look cool! They provide eye protection from bugs, wind, and dust, in addition to ultraviolet rays. Plastic (polycarbonate) lenses are lightweight and the best for safety, although they scratch easily. Specific sport or cycling glasses provide the most comfort and protection, despite giving the wearer a slightly alien appearance.

RAIN JACKET/WINDBREAKER: The choices here are numerous. Waterproof, nonbreathable materials should be avoided since they tend to make it feel like there's a rainstorm of perspiration inside your jacket. Some opt for cape-like rain wear, but we've found these tend to act like a sail when there are windy conditions. Specifically designed cycling jackets work great, are well ventilated and are cut longer in the back to prevent that chilly gap of bare skin. Lightweight rain jackets made of Gore-Tex or other types of waterproof/breathable materials designed for backpacking or hiking are also fine.

LONG UNDERWEAR TOP: For cooler weather. Synthetic is recommended. Long-sleeve cycling jerseys are also nice, though not essential. Avoid cotton.

TIGHTS/LONG UNDERWEAR BOTTOMS: For cold weather. Also must be synthetic. Lycra cross-country ski tights work well.

This is not an all-inclusive listing. Add or delete items depending on the weather and your personal needs.

# Rider's Responsibility

At the time of publication, all of the rides described within these pages were legal. However, due to political pressures, environmental damage, and other mitigating circumstances, any trail may be closed at any time. Please, plan your trip carefully and call ahead to the appropriate agency to determine legality of trails and conditions of their use. Even if described in this book, do not ride on a trail that has been closed to use.

PORTOLA STATE PARK
Star Route 2, La Honda, CA 94020
415-948-9098

BIG BASIN STATE PARK
21600 Big Basin Way
Boulder Creek, CA 95006
408-338-6132

BUTANO STATE PARK
P.O. Box 9
Pescadero, CA 94060
415-879-0173

NISENE MARKS STATE PARK
101 North Big Trees Park Road
Felton, CA 95018
408-335-4598

HENRY COWELL STATE PARK
101 North Big Trees Park Road
Felton, CA 95018
408-335-4598

COYOTE HILLS REGIONAL PARK
11500 Skyline Boulevard
Oakland, CA 94619
510-531-9300

SAN FRANCISCO NATIONAL WILDLIFE REFUGE
P.O. Box 524
Newark, CA 94560
510-792-0222

GRANT RANCH COUNTY PARK
298 Garden Hill Drive
Los Gatos, CA 95030
408-358-3741

HENRY COE STATE PARK
P.O. Box 846
Morgan Hill, CA 95037
408-779-2728

MIDPENINSULA OPEN SPACE DISTRICT
Old Mill Office Center, Bldg. C, Suite 135
201 San Antonio Circle
Mountain View, CA 94040
415-949-5500
*Midpen also puts out a free brochure entitled "Sharing the Trails" that
has excellent guidelines for all trail users. Contact them for a copy.*

EAST BAY REGIONAL PARK DISTRICT
11500 Skyline Boulevard
Oakland, CA 94619
510-531-9300

MOUNT DIABLO STATE PARK
P.O. Box 250
Diablo, CA 94528
510-837-2525

SUGARLOAF STATE PARK
2605 Adobe Canyon Road
Kenwood, CA 95452
707-833-5712

ANNADEL STATE PARK
6201 Channel Drive
Santa Rosa, CA 95409
707-539-3911

GOLDEN GATE NATIONAL RECREATION AREA
Marin Headlands
Fort Cronkhite, CA 94965
415-331-1540

MOUNT TAMALPAIS STATE PARK
Pantoll Ranger Station
801 Panoramic Highway
Mill Valley, CA 94941
415-388-2070

MARIN MUNICIPAL WATER DISTRICT
220 Nellen Avenue
Corte Madera, CA 94925
415-924-4600

POINT REYES NATIONAL SEASHORE
Point Reyes, CA 94956
415-663-1092

SAMUEL P. TAYLOR STATE PARK
P.O. Box 251
Lagunitas, CA 94938
415-488-9897

# Bike Clubs and Trail Organizations

The following is a list of various bicycle clubs and organizations in the Bay Area that work actively to promote responsible land use and access. Through support and active participation, you can help ensure trail preservation and present a unified and responsible image of mountain biking to all.

RESPONSIBLE ORGANIZED MOUNTAIN PEDALERS
P.O. Box 1723
Campbell, CA 95009-1723
408-534-1130

BICYCLE TRIALS COUNCIL OF MARIN
P.O. Box 13842
San Rafael, CA 94913
415-456-7512

BICYCLE TRAILS COUNCIL OF THE EAST BAY
P.O. Box 9583
Berkeley, CA 94709
415-528-BIKE

SANTA CRUZ COUNTY CYCLING CLUB (A.C.T.)
414½ Soquel Avenue
Santa Cruz, CA 93950
408-423-0829

MoMBA (MONTEREY MOUNTAIN BIKE ASSOCIATION)
P.O. Box 51928
Pacific Grove, CA 93950
408-372-2134

WOMBATS (WOMEN'S MTN. BIKING AND TEA SOCIETY)
P.O. Box 757
Fairfax, CA 94930
415-459-0980

IMBA (INTERNATIONAL MOUNTAIN BIKING ASSOCIATION)
P.O. Box 412043
Los Angeles, CA 90041
818-792-8830

TRAIL CENTER
4898 El Camino Real, #205A
Los Altos, CA 94022
415-968-7065

# The Greenbelt of Sanity

We are fortunate to be able to live in a city surrounded by a relative greenbelt of sanity — a collection of parks and preserves dedicated to restoring the mind. These have not occurred accidentally, but have been the product of much hard work, both within the courtroom and on the trail. It seems that some feel undeveloped land is in need of being "improved" by man, be it by bulldozer or trail crew. Imagine the Bay Area without regional or state parks — lands that instead of being open for all of our enjoyment, were tied up as private holdings for the profit of a privileged few.

There is still much open space that is in danger of being sacrificed for development in the form of shopping malls or industrial complexes. Without your help these places may be lost, never to be enjoyed by our children. Imagine if those who came before us never fought to ensure future enjoyment and public access to such beautiful locations as Point Reyes, Mount Diablo, or Wildcat Canyon. Following is a list of organizations, both grass roots and national that need your help in the form of money, volunteer time, or even a few moments spent writing a card to senators or congressmen. Please help to ensure that others will also be able to enjoy our greenbelt.

GREEN BELT ALLIANCE
116 New Montgomery, Suite 640
San Francisco, CA 94105
415-543-4291

TRUST FOR PUBLIC LAND
116 New Montgomery
San Francisco, CA 94105
415-495-4014

RESTORING THE EARTH
1713 C Martin Luther King Jr. Boulevard
Berkeley, CA 94709
415-843-2645

NATURE CONSERVANCY
74103 Market Street, Third Floor
San Francisco, CA 94103
415-777-0487

## About the Authors

Michael Hodgson is an Outdoor Writer's Association award-winning journalist and author of seven books. Michael writes a weekly column for the *San Jose Mercury News'* Venture Section. Michael also writes as a technical editor for *Outdoor Retailer Magazine* and a contributing editor for *Backpacker Magazine*.

Mark Lord's outdoor experience spans more than twenty years. He has guided clients in the mountains of North America, Europe, and New Zealand and has extensively cycle-toured in the U.S. and Canada. He is also the author of a guide book to cross-country skiing in Lake Tahoe. Mark is currently the Director of Outdoor Programs for Catalyst Consulting, a Santa Cruz–based experiential training and development firm. He lives with his family in Aptos, California.

# MORE OUTDOOR GUIDES
# From Western Tanager Press. . .

## Bicycling Country Roads ☐
*By Joanne Rife*

All the beauty of California between San Jose and Santa Barbara is just a bike ride away in *Bicycling Country Roads*. This handy guidebook describes 50 bicycle trips in the region. The trips vary from 10 to 70 miles, and each is accompanied by photographs and a route map.

*Illus., Maps, 124 pp., 6 X 9, Paper. $9.95 (ISBN 0-934136-16-5)*

## Hidden Walks in the Bay Area ☐
*By Stephen Altschuler*

A walking guide to hidden, natural places in the San Francisco Bay Area. Included are 25 loop walks between one and three miles, in Berkeley, Oakland, Kensington, Mill Valley, Albany and Sausalito. The Author takes the walker past creeks, waterfalls, and redwood groves, as well as many magnificent old homes. Essays or historical vignettes, included with each walk, encourage walkers to reflect upon their present experience and offer insight inot the rch history of the Bay Area neighborhoods.

*Illus., Maps, 180 pp., 5 X 8, Paper, $9.95 (ISBN 0-934136-43-2)*

## More Hidden Walks in the Bay Area ☐
*by Stephen Altschuler*

In this companion volume, Altschuler reveals more secret places to explore in the Bay Area. A walking guide to often overlooked places in the San Francisco area, this volume contains one to five mile loop walks in San Francisco, Berkeley, Oakland, Piedmont, Pt. Richmond, Larkspur, Corte Madera, Ross, San Anselmo, San Rapahel, Sausalito, and Alameda. Each walk provides directions, a map, and numerous architectural, botanical and historical notes.

*Illus., Maps, 200 pp., 5 X 8, Paper, $9.95 (ISBN 0-934136-48-3)*

Western Tanager Press
1111 Pacific Avenue
Santa Cruz, CA 95060
(408) 425-1112    FAX (408) 425-0171

Please send me the titles I have indicated above. I am enclosing $_____. (Please include $1.50 for shipping. California residents, please include sales tax.) Send check or money order. For Visa and Mastercard orders, please include card number and expiration date. Our catalog is available upon request.

Name_____

Address_____

Visa/MC#_____